Bury
MY HEART
AT
W.H.SMITH'S

BURY MY HEART AT W.H.SMITH'S

BRIAN ALDISS

A Writing Life

Hodder & Stoughton

LONDON SYDNEY AUCKLAND TORONTO

British Library Cataloguing in Publication Data

Aldiss, Brian W. (Brian Wilson) *1925-*
Bury my heart at W. H. Smith's.
1. Fiction in English. Aldiss, Brian W. (Brian Wilson),
1925-
I. Title
823.914

ISBN 0-340-53661-6

First published in Great Britain 1990

Published by Hodder and Stoughton,
a division of Hodder and Stoughton Ltd,
Mill Road, Dunton Green, Sevenoaks, Kent TN13 2YA.
Editorial Office: 47 Bedford Square, London WC1B 3DP.

Photoset by E.P.L. BookSet, Norwood, London.

Printed in Great Britain by Biddles Ltd, Guildford
and Kings Lynn.

Although these pages necessarily
exclude the family
they are dedicated
to the family
and in particular
to
WENDY and MARK

The Boy shrugs. "A poet's work," he answers. "To name the unnameable, to point at frauds, to take sides, start arguments, shape the world and stop it from going to sleep." And if rivers of blood flow from the cuts his verses inflict, then they will nourish him.

Salman Rushdie, *The Satanic Verses*

CONTENTS

Apéritif
Bury my Heart at W. H. Smith's

The train was crossing India from west to east. It ran steadily over the wide Ganges plain, from Agra towards Jamalpur, the weight of the brilliant day bearing down upon its carriages. I stared out of the window, stared and stared, absorbed in the landscape.

Nothing was to be seen but the wastes of the plain and the sky above it. A tree, a thatched hut, stood here or there, as pallid as the earth itself. In that dry season, there was no sign of the river; it had dwindled like a shrivelled limb.

Peasants worked on the plain, sometimes near the tracks, sometimes distantly. Unlike the peasants of China, these were isolated one from another. The sun had burned them hollow. They toiled almost naked. Some stood upright, working with hoes, while others were bent double. They appeared motionless, like figures on a frieze.

And they laboured on the plain every day of their lives.

Monotony was their lot. How did a man's thoughts run, out there on the baked mud? What would he have to tell at sunset?

"I was up before dawn and took a handful of rice. Then I worked, as you know. It was hot. Nothing grows. Now I shall rest. It's dark. I will sleep . . . "

That terrible monotony, as stern a ruler as the sun. Ever since infancy I had feared reincarnation when, at the age of three, I was convinced I had been a wizard burned at the stake in a previous incarnation; the agony of the fire often woke me, crying. What was there to prevent me from awakening next time as a peasant, bound to the Ganges?

To survive as an Indian peasant requires endurance born of centuries of fatalistic courage, passive acceptance, qualities scarce in the unsleeping West.

Those days on the train were ones in which my determination to be a writer developed. I wished to tell everyone about that alien way of life. I had my subject matter. What I did not realise was that I also had the stubborn temperament a writer requires.

A glance at the list of titles I have written since those Indian days shows a preoccupation with time. From *Space, Time and Nathaniel*, to *Non-Stop*, through *Moment of Eclipse* and *Eighty-Minute Hour*, to *Seasons in Flight* and *Forgotten Life*, the idea of passing time glides like a serpent through the words.

Of course it was never planned that way. It just happened, as much in life happens. Perhaps I have a problem with my time sense.

Whatever creativity is, it is in part a solution to a problem.

LENINGRAD. I was one of six writers on an Arts Council tour of the Soviet Union. We had been to Moscow and flown over the Caucasus to Tbilisi. Now we were being taken to the Kirov ballet.

The home of the Kirov is a grandly restored eighteenth-century building. The company itself is magnificent.

That night, they were dancing *Hamlet* to a modern score.

The ballet stayed very close to Shakespeare's original story. But even a faithful *Hamlet* becomes, without words, the story of two rather pleasant middle-aged people who marry and, on their honeymoon in Elsinore, are pestered by a young fellow in black. This adolescent, contrary to the usual rule of adolescence, loves his father, who has died, and spends all evening dancing in and out, mucking up the honeymoon.

Hamlet is not *Hamlet* without Shakespeare's words. The best part of a writer exists on the printed page. Without his or her words, a writer spends his time dancing in and out, imprisoned in Elsinore.

BORNEO. If there are still white patches on the globe, then unsurveyed parts of the interior of Borneo must qualify as *terra incognita*. There, hiding from the depredations of the timber industry, lives a wandering tribe which regards itself as part of the jungle which encloses it.

This tribe has a religion which would interest Carl Jung. It believes that all men possess two souls, an ordinary everyday soul which deals with ordinary everyday life, and a second soul the tribe calls the Dream Wanderer. This Dream Wanderer is a free being, not under the command of the person it inhabits. Although it cannot manage everyday things, it is native in the lands beyond the prosaic.

Directly I heard of this tribe, I knew I was an honorary member. I also am inhabited by a Dream Wanderer. The Wanderer roams where it will; sometimes it leans over my shoulder when I am typing and communicates in its own fashion. If I am lucky.

Writers must fortify themselves with pride and egotism as best they can. The process is analogous to using sandbags and loose timbers to protect a house against flood. Writers are vulnerable creatures like anyone else. For what do they have in reality? Not sandbags, not timbers. Just a flimsy reputation and a name . . .

She was very attractive and we were getting on famously. By mutual consent we crept away from the party and found ourselves in a little warm courtyard. There we fell into intense talk, touching, and looking deep into each other's eyes. The point came when I had to tell her I was a writer of novels.

"Do you write under your own name?" she asked.

CHAPTER 1

My First Editor

Arundel Street is a short steep street leading down from the Strand to the Victoria Embankment and the Thames. If you drove down it in a car with bad brakes, you might end up in the river.

On this occasion, I was going down it on foot, slowly and cautiously. I was about to meet my first editor.

Just recently, I went down Arundel Street again, thirty years later. Much had changed. Dull concrete frontages loom where once there was fanciful brick and terracotta. Colour has gone. There are large corporations, who like concrete frontages, where once small companies clustered behind flettons.

In the fifties, there were basement windows through which a passer-by glimpsed various activities. I peered through protective railings on this momentous occasion to glimpse a tall figure in shirtsleeves who was talking and laughing.

I ascended four shallow steps, where a brass plate announced "Maclaren Books, Nova Publications". I entered, and made my way down into the basement.

A long room had been made complex by an arrangement of desks, cupboards, boxes, piles of books and magazines, pin-ups on walls as if it were still wartime, and several men, sitting or bustling about.

I was a callow youth, yet not entirely callow and not en-

14

tirely youthful. Over the previous Christmas, the Christmas of 1955, I had won the short story competition in the *Observer*, then the leading Sunday paper. The story was set in the year 2500 AD and entitled "Not For an Age".

Now I met my first editor. His name was Ted Carnell, the great EJ, whose obituary I would write, many years later, for *The Times*.

Ted always dressed neatly and was courteous and pleasant. He lived in a neat little house in Plumstead and spoke with a genial Cockney accent.

He had already accepted two stories from me, "Criminal Record" and "Outside". He was about to take me out to lunch and solicit more stories from me.

Think of all those literary anecdotes about poets meeting Cyril Connolly or Robert Ross for the first time. I was meeting Ted Carnell.

Before we left for the restaurant, he put on his jacket and showed me a watercolour painting by the Irish artist Gerald Quinn. It depicted some enigmatic metal shapes lying on a beach under an orange sky. It was very accomplished. I liked it immediately.

"Do you think it would be better with a human figure?" Ted asked.

"Worse."

"It's marvellous. I was thinking of running a competition for the best story explaining what the pic is all about."

Although the competition never materialised, Quinn's painting appeared on the cover of *New Worlds*. It still looks good.

The restaurant turned out to be an ABC in High Holborn. We went downstairs, where Ted had a regular table and was on good terms with the waitress.

"How are the bunions, Mary, dear?" Ted asked.

"Not so bad today, thanks, Ted, how's yourself? I'm saving two bits of the plum pie for you. It's very nice and going fast."

I was disappointed. Did Sartre have similar exchanges with

the waitresses on the Left Bank?

Over lunch, Ted expressed an admiration for my stories and confidence in my future career. He wanted more stories for both his magazines. Perhaps one day, he added, I would like to meet John Wyndham?

John Murray to Currer Bell: "Perhaps one day you'd care to meet Charles Dickens?"

How many times have I been up to London since then? Living only an hour's train ride from London, I have never seriously contemplated moving to the capital. As a result, a little excitement remains whenever I get aboard a Paddington-bound train.

Of course I was sorry that Ted was not grander, more aspiring, and that his waitress had bunions. But there had been the sight of the Gerald Quinn.

This is what I was doing with myself at that time when I did not dare to call myself a writer.

I wrote in the evenings, when possible. For all of the day, I worked in an Oxford bookshop.

What I felt inwardly was that I was undergoing a sort of personal renaissance. Overloaded with books and prints, that shabby little bookshop seemed the richest in the world. Its dust was hallowed.

This is what it looked like to my innocent 1947 eye.

The name over the shop says *Sanders & Co.* It also says Salutation House; there was once an inn of that name on the site. The shop is situated in Oxford's High Street, nearly opposite St Mary the Virgin Church. The shilling shelves are on the left as you enter.

Hang on. In the shilling shelves are many books, all at that magic price, some of them worth a deal more to the right buyer. When the shop closes, someone staggers out of the shop with a huge black shutter which locks over the front of the shelves. Me.

This was the first job I did at Sanders. At the interview with

16

the old man, he asked, "When would you be prepared to start?"

"Now?" I asked.

"Now," he said. I was set to tidying the shilling shelves. I remember one of the books I tidied, that first afternoon. It was *Lalla Rookh* by Tom Moore, a friend of Byron's. Time was when no self-respecting home was without a copy of *Lalla Rookh*. Many editions came off the mills, some bound in Russian leather, padded with cotton wool.

Moore was a jolly man, ever prepared to sing for his supper, and he had a sharp, observant eye, as his diaries show. Sad to say, many copies of *Lalla Rookh* went out to Sanders' shilling shelves during my time there. Every dog his day . . .

A rich but chastening environment for a budding author is a bookshop.

Sanders' shop is a long narrow dark secretive overstocked gallimaufry of a bookshop, comparing unfavourably in roominess with the crew quarters of one of Nelson's ships. Packed under its low beams is a profusion of ill-sorted stock. From folios to duodecimos, an impressive range of volumes presents itself or lurks in obscurity.

Nor are there only books here. Maps, prints, engravings, hang wherever there is space. These are Sanders' specialities. The old maps – Speeds, Saxtons, Mordens – mainly of the English counties, mop up what light filters in from outside while remaining themselves beautiful, cryptic, and severe in their Hogarth frames. The elegance of those frames!

Halfway towards the rear of the shop is a door which gives on to a twisting stair which leads up to Mr Sanders' office and, beyond that, the rare book room where few are allowed to go. On the staircase is a framed engraving of Dr Johnson short-sightedly reading a 32mo.

Mind your head as we get to the rear compartment of the shop downstairs. Here, besides rows of books small and gigantic, such as Mrs Jekyll's Country Life books, we come to the stove, a desk, a gate cutting off the cellar, and the till.

The till is a wooden affair with a narrow slot in its top, through which one may write on a roll of paper

Ensor's England . . . . 1. 1. 0.

The till opens with a *ting*, the paper drum rolls on, and the assistant deposits a guinea in the correct wooden partitions.

Above the till is a window which allows a ration of light into this section of the shop, although the ration is so feeble that electric lights burn all day. The window is partly obscured by an old hurdy-gurdy which hangs there. It is Italian, and has to be tucked under the chin like a violin and wound by a small handle. Occasionally, Sanders, a music-lover, will take it down and play a melody.

Oh, yes, a strong whiff of the nineteenth century still clings to Sanders' shop. This is the first taste I have had of England since I was a child when, at seventeen, I was swallowed up into the British Army. I am intoxicated by the strangeness of everything. I half-read all the books, flitting from one to another, while at the same time dreaming my private dreams of sex and science fiction.

Beyond the hurdy-gurdy is a last section, filled in part by a small office and a packing booth. The books here, tucked at the rear of the shop, are of less tempting varieties. This is the resort of Classical textbooks, Agriculture and Logic. There is also a narrow space behind the Classics, very unpopular with assistants, in which some stationery is housed: the humdrum things that students need, particularly the students from Oriel College, next to the shop, such as loose-leaf books, refills for same, pencils, notebooks, and the like.

In the office sits Mrs Y. In the packing booth stands Mr Watts.

I bring in a book for despatch abroad.

"That 'on't go today," says Mr Watts.

Although this is not all Mr Watts says, it is possibly his most characteristic utterance. Watts is a kindly, crusty man, with teeth of fierce yellow and a tisicking cough, both cough and yellowness caught from the old pipe he constantly smokes. Uncomplainingly, he works all day with paper and string, making the odd excursion to the post office in St Aldate's, or delivering a package to a college nearby. His movements as he works are leisurely and professional. He never wastes an inch of string.

After about four in the afternoon, when a sort of drowse overcomes the shop in general, as the lack of air gets to us all, and Mrs Y makes a pot of tea for us, Mr Watts views further candidates for posting with an increasingly jaundiced eye and larger clouds of smoke, and utters again his immortal phrase, "That 'on't go today."

Beyond Mr Watts' cubbyhole is a door into the rear premises. The shelves here are rather makeshift, stuffed with books in wild disorder, books bought cheap and unloved. They lie now, idle and unemployed, volumes on brass and beadwork and brassica crops and ballet and the breaststroke and Bastien-Lepage and Brittany and Buckingham, to venture no further into the alphabet.

Even this is not the end of everything. There are rickety back stairs, where once the maids of the Salutation Inn carried up trays of porter to gentlemen dining privately in upper rooms. On the stairs, on every step, more books are piled, right up to the top. They are making their way upstairs. There is hope for them. Some will enjoy the privilege of being catalogued by that shy, charming, poetic man you probably meet just here. He is polite, amusing, and already a little bald. He is just the company a new assistant wants, and is recently down from Merton. His name is Roger Lancelyn Green.

Roger is no more. At that time, he had written a delicate fantasy or two, some poems, and a book on Andrew Lang. He was destined to become quite famous and to marry a pleasant Oxford lady. Later would come his involvement with Lewis Carroll. At present we will leave him cataloguing books on the stairs and peering into a first edition of Douglas Jerrold's *Mrs*

Caudle's Curtain Lectures, which were at that time still sought after in Oxford.

If we turned left past Roger, we should enter the rare book store behind Mr Sanders' office. Instead, we turn right where the stair twists, and find ourselves in Heaven.

This is the highest part of the ancient building, highest and untidiest. Its one dusty window looks out across the broken rooftops of Oxford.

In imitation of the real thing, Heaven is damp and leaky. Here, Dickensian charm and creative vandalism go hand-in-hand.

Many are the old books which find their way into Sanders' clutches. Some are fashion or natural history books. Some are of a topographical nature, illustrated by steel engravings or etchings: views of English countryside, foreign views, views of Oxford colleges. Sometimes the bindings of such volumes may be torn. Sometimes the text may be considered dull. Then the book can be broken up and the illustrations or maps sold separately. And sold especially well when coloured and mounted. This applies with particular force to that beautiful octavo book in three volumes, Ingram's *Memorials of Oxford*, many sets of which, entering the premises of Salutation House, find themselves broken up for the sake of the engravings of colleges within. Good complete sets must by now be extremely scarce.

The breaking, the mounting, the colouring, is done in Heaven. Here, at benches under a dusty window, sit Sheila and Miss Worms, working away with their watercolours. Mr Rudolph Ackermann's Repository of the Arts, which produced many fine illustrated books last century, must have been just such a place as Heaven, housing folk who had fled from the Terror in France after the Revolution. We find an echo of that here in Heaven: the cheerful and teasing Miss Worms is in fact a refugee from Hitler's Reich. As for Sheila, she is young and pert and pretty, and I once fancied myself in love with her.

So to the stock room behind Sanders' office. Here are the scarcest books, the most precious, the most cherished. The stock room is subdivided. In a small locked room called Pickle rest those books deemed most scarce, most precious, most cherished, by the miserly Sanders. These regal favourites are drawn up in ranks, *gaining in value* . . . We mentioned Mr Ackermann; here stand no fewer than seventeen sets of Ackermann's *History of Oxford*, in two volumes, full of lovely coloured plates of colleges. There are even a few sets of Ackermann's *Cambridge*. Together with many other books, some mildly pornographic, which Sanders could not bear to sell.

In the stock room you may come across a set of Peacock's novels in tree-calf, or a complete set of Thomas Hardy's first editions, all bound uniform (but this is vandalism) in blue buckram, together with many other prizes. In huge wooden cases, specially made by Mr Watts, are stored Hogarth's engravings of London life and Piranesi's engravings of prisons and of Rome, in various states. There are also some Rowlandsons. Such Rowlandsons! Country scenes, bawdy scenes, inns, maidens, stage coaches, the whole eighteenth-century world which Thomas Rowlandson's calligraphic line so skilfully evoked.

I had never heard of Rowlandson until I went into Mr Sanders' stock room, and have worshipped the man's work ever since. He was unrivalled as a draughtsman until Beardsley drew. In Mr Sanders' house on the Woodstock Road hung perhaps ten lilting Rowlandsons, country landscapes of the greatest delicacy of line and colour. No doubt they are now in the Paul Mellon collection. Over Sanders' mantelpiece hung a pristine print of the painting generally regarded as Rowlandson's masterpiece, "Vauxhall Gardens".

As far as Rowlandson is known, he is valued for his scenes of bawdy, of boisterousness and drinking bouts. But with that subject matter goes a style of transparent delicacy. His creamy young Georgian maids might have stepped out of *Cranford* or a novel by Thomas Hardy. A travelling print-seller used to come round and sell Sanders pornographic Rowlandsons for his gentlemen clients.

Without being judgmental, Thomas Rowlandson elegantly recorded an England at once awful and enviable. I owe my introduction to him to Frank Sanders – another amusing bounder.

Three Pounds a Week

Two people served with me in the shop. One and a half to be precise. The half was Mrs Y, who did the accounts as well as serving, and so was generally tucked away in the downstairs office. She was always ready to emerge for a chat. If she was asked for a book by a customer, Mrs Y would fall into a mild, ladylike panic. With one finger up to her lip, she would go slowly round in circles, cooing, "Oh, dear, have we got that now, I wonder? *What* an interesting question. Where would it be, I wonder? What did you say the title was again?", until Bill Oliver or I rescued her.

Bill Oliver had been a scholar of St John's College, and had served with the Eighth Army in the desert. Now he wore a blue suit and a large ginger moustache, over which his grey eyes bulged in accusatory fashion. He looked ferocious, yet I never met a milder man. He worked long hours without complaint. He was married to a distinguished, smiling, foreign lady, relation, it was said, of Robert Musil, author of *The Man Without Qualities* – a novel I never managed to get through, despite the local connection.

In those days, following the war and paper-rationing, there was a scarcity of books, with the consequence that everybody wanted them. The shop, at least during the university term, was always full of people asking for books we did not have. We sold a small number of new books; but those were often rationed by the publishers.

The representative for Oxford University Press was a tall thin man called Mr Lathom. He had a face like a kind lemon, his expression fostered by the number of times he had to say no as gently as possible. If we ordered six copies of the *Shorter Oxford English Dictionary* for the beginning of term, we would be lucky to get one. At that time shortages were a way of life.

All the staff in Sanders got along well together, which was fortunate, since we worked long hours. I had to be there at a quarter to nine. I had an hour and a half for lunch. The shop closed at five thirty, but we were expected to work until at least six thirty, often seven. Many a time it was eight. That was the worst of Sanders, that and the pay.

At five thirty, Sanders would come down from his office, smoking his pipe, to see that everything was secure, shutters up and door locked. We would all light cigarettes and "get down to the real work".

Frank Sanders was a small vigorous man with a perky face and a quiff of white hair. He resembled Max Beerbohm's caricature of Arnold Bennett. He was a humorous man and in many ways a terrible crook; he kept us destitute and laughing.

Sanders was sincere in certain matters. His love of music, books and Rowlandson could not be faulted. He also had the gift of the gab, and this led him into areas of insincerity.

Middle-aged ladies flocked to Sanders, just as they flocked to the lectures of C. S. Lewis, who was then at Magdalen College and occasionally came into the shop. The ladies tried to charm Frank Sanders, but Frank Sanders always charmed the ladies more. Wives of heads of colleges were his natural victims. In the course of intimate conversations, when the ladies were led up to his office, books and money would change hands, valuable prints would turn into more valuable cheques. Sanders would then escort the ladies to the door with amiable courtesy.

Directly they had gone, the mask would fall. He would

stamp back into the rear of the shop. "Oh, that Lady – ! How she talks, how she wastes my time. I can't bear the woman. She's humbug all through . . . "

Frank Sanders was a self-made man. He began with no advantages in life, beyond the resources of his brain. As a youth in North Devon he sold newspapers for W. H. Smith on Barnstaple railway station. I too once lived in Barnstaple; this gave us something in common, and allowed him the opportunity to pay me less than I was worth.

The gift of the gab brought more than middle-aged ladies to Sanders. It brought some of the famous as well. I squinted up from street level at these leviathans of the literary scene. Hugh Macdonald, editor of Marvell's poems and other works, always grumpy, but fun to imitate behind his back. Geoffrey Grigson, poet, producer of books, never satisfied with our service. Many celebrated dons, the most engaging of whom was probably J. I. M. Stewart. Stewart was busy installing himself in Christ Church when I arrived in my shabby suit to conquer Oxford. He was writing a series of Shakespearian or mock-Shakespearian plays for the BBC Third Programme, then at its cultural zenith. Years later, Stewart must have felt a little rueful when he found Tom Stoppard tilling the same ground more profitably in *Rosencrantz and Guildenstern are Dead*. But by then he was well embarked on his second or third career as detective writer Michael Innes.

On a Saturday afternoon, when Oxford fell into a comfortable doze, and those who wished to curl up with a good book were already doing so, A. V. Bond entered Sanders.

He descended from somewhere called "The Cotswolds". I put the term in quotation marks because I knew no more of the Cotswolds than the name; I had never been there. Mr Bond called himself "The Poet of the Cotswolds".

He was roughly dressed, garbed generally in a long black coat wrapped tight round his wiry frame, as if he were about to be shipped to Patagonia, where warmth counts for more than style. To me, he was the Ancient of Days, or at least of an

25

Afternoon, his sparse white hair tormented by the memory of Cotswold typhoons – or whatever they had up there – a straggly white beard, and piercing blue eyes.

Mr Bond was dramatic. He entered the shop like a thinned-down Wolfit, one arm raised in salute, and immediately began to talk. His chief target was Mrs Y, who eagerly devoured his every word. She would sit with legs crossed, elbows propped on desk, and hands clasped under her chin, looking up at him as if to convey visually the message that Earth, and the Cotswolds in particular, had not anything to show more fair than Mr Bond.

I too was fascinated. It was my first poet. He would declaim in the shop, and Mrs Y would clap prettily, and say afterwards, "Of course he's such an amusing man and so *gifted*."

His poems were printed by Mr Vincent, a local printer with a shop in King Edward Street, and sold at a penny a time. I remember none of his poems, unless he was guilty of a sonnet beginning "The heart in wonder like a lonely wren . . . " I have retained none of his little sheets, unfortunately.

Mr Sanders once told Mr Bond a dirty joke, which profoundly shocked him. He left the shop, returned to the Cotswolds, and did not reappear for a month.

His open-air aspect convinced me that he must inhabit a mountainside, and a gorse bush he had made comfortable. I was disappointed later both by the extreme couthness of the Cotswolds – which resemble burial mounds more than mountains – and the discovery that the poet lived in Stow-on-the-Wold. I'm sure he was designed for the Pennines at least or, failing that, the Quantocks.

The visitor I liked least was Evelyn Waugh.

Waugh I observed with a particular interest. At school, we had been taught English by a fine product of Trinity College Dublin, H. C. Fay. Fay, known as Crasher after the sound of his hobnailed boots which he wore at all times, modelled himself on George Bernard Shaw, and had something of Shaw's wit. His wit was sharp. It was truthful. It often transfixed us. But there was no malice behind it. We liked it. And we admired Fay – less because of his learning than because he had once, in class, told us that his cat was too fat to climb through her door hole into the house because she was pregnant again.

Sensation! The word "pregnant" had never been spoken by an adult in our presence before. Fay was treating us like human beings. We were grateful. From then on, we were on Fay's side, and content to be transfixed regularly by his wit.

His virtues consisted in more than the possession of a pregnant cat. He was sympathetic to my wish to become a writer. In his class, I was granted a privilege. Instead of a weekly essay, Crasher Fay allowed me to write a weekly story. While the rest of them were turning out their constipated page and a half on "My Visit to the Dentist", or "Why I Love Rugger", or "How to Treat a Hotwater Bottle", I could plunge into the real thing. Imagination.

Fay was indulgent about the stories he received, though they were more fantastic and would-be humorous than he liked. One Monday morning in class, his patience stretched to breaking point. He seized up the story I had submitted and waved it furiously in the air.

"Aldiss," he said, "if you do not mend your ways, you are going to end up as a second Evelyn Waugh."

I blushed the colour of ambition.

Waugh's early novels were pure delight. Meeting Waugh in the flesh was a different matter, at least if one was victim material, a bookseller's assistant. As I remember him, Waugh was always in a bad mood. Perhaps it was because he was writing *Brideshead Revisited*, which is where he went off the gold standard. Later, Waugh redeemed himself a hundredfold with *The Ordeal of Gilbert Pinfold*, a brave, funny and perceptive book. Largely autobiographical, I understand.

He entered Sanders like some minor devil, small, bounderish, rosy on the wrong bits of cheek, with a smell not of brimstone but an equally noxious mixture of cigars and lavender water. He wished to see Mr Sanders – so imperiously wished to see Mr Sanders that anyone less than Mr Sanders was hardly worth a glance. A flick of the cigar was all we could hope for.

Sanders would appear in his usual genial way and sweep Waugh upstairs. They would emerge later, Waugh clutching some luxuriously bound volume of landscape engravings, both laughing. I believe he once had a very nice Boydell's *Thames* from Sanders. They would part at the door, glowing false bonhomie on both sides. Waugh was a bad payer. And inaccurate with his cigar ash.

John Betjeman was much more pleasant. He would arrive giggling and steaming in an old coat with a fur collar which might once have done duty for Bud Flanagan. His hair was curly and somewhat enveloped in an old felt hat. He filled the shop with formidable goodwill, made himself pleasant to all, and signed a copy of his poems for me.

"Such an interesting man," cooed Mrs Y, after one of his appearances. "And so fond of Oxford. He's like me, he *loves* beauty."

Betjeman came not to buy but to sell. He was then living near Wantage. He reviewed for the now defunct *Daily Herald*, where he was bombarded with the very sweepings of publishers' lists. Why they sent him such rubbish I do not know, unless Bloomsbury had an exceptionally poor view of the *Daily Herald*. The gaudier the cover, the more likely it was to be despatched to Wantage and a labouring Betjeman.

But Frank Sanders would be all smiles, and would go out into the High Street with Betjeman, to look in his van.

Reader, this is not mere anecdotage, please. You are being treated to social history. (Besides, what if *Summoned by Bells* should, in another century, rank with Moore's *Lalla Rookh*? In his day, some good judges placed Betjeman among our best English poets, with his touching mixture of dread, humour and inspired pedestrianism). Stop and consider the implications behind that last paragraph.

Betjeman drove up the High in his old van and stopped outside Sanders. He then came into the shop for a half-hour's chat, after which he strolled out again with Sanders. We are talking about 1950.

A little amplification of the point. I was a success at Sanders. After less than a year there, Sanders allowed me to dress the window every Monday. We mixed antiquarian, second-hand and new books, perhaps on a theme. Natural History, say. Bill Oliver wrote the tickets in his neat hand.

Dressing the window was enjoyable; from there we could watch the academic world go by. Every Monday morning, a tubby old man with white hair and a carnation in his button-hole would come up the High from Magdalen College. He pushed a barrel-organ, stopping every so often to play an air. From Sanders' window, you could hear him as far away as Halliday's Antiques.

Despite my limited hours for personal pursuits, I was keeping company with the most beautiful girl in Oxford. Her name was Pam, and her hair was a staggering mixture of sunlight, ginger and Pre-Raphaelite red. She liked – we liked between us – the old Neapolitan tune, "Come Back to Sorrento".

The barrel-organ man (I knew his name once) would trundle his barrel-organ up the High, stopping outside Sanders to play "Come Back to Sorrento". Methinks that music hath a dying *ping*. I would climb from the window and pay him lavishly. Sixpence. A sizeable fraction of the three pounds which was my weekly wage. What sentiment! What music! What generosity!

What happiness.

Try parking your barrel-organ, or your van, outside Sanders now.

In those days, children, there were no double yellow lines up the High. Indeed, there was scarcely any traffic. Old Oxford, breathing the last enchantments of the Middle Ages, expired in a death rattle of traffic wardens.

Oh, it sounds great. If you were content to work till seven

29

every evening for three pounds a week. Of course, if you knew you were going to be famous (a secret kept from all but Pam and Mrs Y), that made everything OK.

So there stood Betjeman's old van, full of trashy books. Sanders would turn them over and finally say, "A fiver, John?"

"Well, I know it's rubbish, Frank, but someone must read the stuff. I really have to buy a new set of tyres. Couldn't you make it ten pounds?"

They soon came to an agreement.

The agreement was five pounds.

Bill and I then carried the books into the shop. Betjeman departed.

Sanders kept any books that were at all passable, merging them with our new stock. The rest of the books were crammed into two large suitcases. These suitcases I took up to Foyle's bookshop in London, where the buyer in the basement would pay me perhaps twenty pounds.

The only novel I can remember salvaging from Betjeman's collections was Guy Endore's *Methinks the Lady*, which I read avidly while immersed at the same time in Pope's poems and Lewis Mumford's *Condition of Man*. I still read several books at once.

This rather shady dealing in review books stood me in good stead later, when I became literary editor of the *Oxford Mail*.

Christmases at Bill and Gertrude Oliver's house were different from ordinary English ones. The food shortage was noticeable. We ate Smarties at intervals. The Christmas tree was decorated in the Austrian way. Its tip reached the ceiling, and it was loaded all the way up in white candles, nothing but white candles. It resembled a dancing girl in an inflammable white dress. The heat was terrific. We had to back away. Yet the house stands till this day.

Bill is dead. He died young, of cancer. When I went to see him in hospital, he would talk of nothing but bookselling. I tried to lure him to more personal subjects. He would not be moved. His talk was purely of books, new and old, and the problems of selling them. He was a most impersonal man; a door had been locked which even terminal illness did not open.

During his time with the Eighth Army in North Africa, Bill had been captured by the Italians – a fate given to few, I imagine. He spoke a little Italian, and so had been made interpreter, in which role he was allowed some freedom in the camp, between prisoners and captors.

Thus he was able to get his hands on the supplies of tea which the International Red Cross sent British prisoners. Because of a severe tea shortage among Mussolini's heroes, the commodity was highly prized and could be exchanged for Italian cigarettes. The British POWs, despite their fondness for tea, did not drink it, preferring to trade. Bill, with access to the stores, found a solution to the dilemma.

He would take the boxes of tea one at a time to his fellows. They would have a brew-up, dry the tea leaves afterwards and pack the used leaves back in the boxes, which Bill would then return to their proper place in the store. After which they were traded for cigarettes. Everyone was happy.

One day, the Italians got a jump ahead. The British were forced to trade virgin tea for the cigarettes. Next day, the Italian camp commandant had his prisoners on parade and asked them sternly who had been messing about and ruining the new tea ration.

Good work, Bill.

Sunday tea with Mrs Y was pretty eccentric. Her name was Mrs Yashimoto. As far as I can piece together the story, she had gone out to Japan as a young missionary. There she met and fell in love with Mr Yashimoto, and married him. A rash and romantic thing to do – just before the USA and Britain declared war on Japan.

For the crime of marrying a foreign woman, Mr Yashimoto was interned. His wife somehow managed to escape and returned to England. She led a devout Christian life, pining all the while for her husband. Many looked down on her, since the Japanese – long before they started to shower little electronic goodies upon us – were hated at the time.

Eventually Mrs Y got her husband back. To the delight and benefit of them both.

By then I was preparing to leave Sanders.

I had asked Sanders several times for a rise in pay. He refused. What he dangled instead was the possibility of a partnership in the business when he retired, which, I was given to understand, might be any day.

Then he said to me, taking me aside, "You come up and see me on a Friday evening, and I'll slip you an extra pound. You're worth it. Just don't tell anyone else."

"No, I'm sorry, I couldn't accept it on those terms."

This annoyed him. After work that evening, I took Bill to the nearby Blue Boar Inn. Over a pint, I told him my tale. Bill was completely unmoved. "Yes, Frank made me the same offer. I turned it down on the same grounds you did."

"What about the partnership?"

"That's complete boloney. I've heard that tale too. Everyone hears it. The man is a hypocrite."

"Christ, worse than that, I'd say."

"I would prefer to categorise him as a hypocrite. The man has had a hard life."

After that, there seemed nothing for it but to leave.

Vienna Steak, Heinz Salad Cream

Sanders liked his pint of blood. When he finally retired, he sold the shop, as it happened, to a friend of mine, Kyril Bonfiglioli. By then I had gone.

Those first years in Oxford were a time of intense dark living. I had to come to terms with many incompatibilities. The shop with its desperately long hours was a prison, yet it was also a magic cave, an inspiration, jostling with the personalities of dead authors.

Outside was freedom, of a kind. I was the underprivileged poor, living in a rented room, with little spare time and the crazed impulse to write. Behind everything was the East, which I was sickening for and trying to forget, knowing I should never be able to return there.

The room in which I lodged was on the second floor of a house in King Edward Street owned by a Miss Pond, a learned and sickly lady who taught Spanish and Latin. Even the landladies were learned in Oxford.

It was curious to realise that I knew nothing of England. I had taken part in World War II, one of the biggest initiation rites in history. Here I was at the age of twenty-three, trying to write, trying not to be a savage.

In that dark shop, I missed the sun. Life in the East had mainly been spent outdoors, in the glorious light of the tropics. No wonder *Non-Stop* concerns people trapped for ever inside the confines of a spaceship going nowhere. This is the metaphorical way in which science fiction is truthful, and has less to do with science than the emotions.

Involved in the bookshop, I became involved to some extent with the university, for which I had, at that time, great respect. Some of my friends were undergraduates, such as Jack Bentley, with whom I had worked in the signal office in Hong Kong. Jack spent a lot of his time in his rooms, reading Thorne Smith. He never took to Balliol.

One of the pleasures on offer was the college play. Most of the colleges had active dramatic clubs; St John's had the St John's Mummers, and so forth. At the apex of the college clubs was OUDS, the university dramatic society.

All the clubs performed old plays, particularly plays set for the English curriculum. Merton did *Julius Caesar* in modern dress, Nazi uniform. It was the first time I had heard of such creative parachronism.

It was possible to see plays which are a fundamental part of English literature but rarely performed, such as Kyd's *The Spanish Tragedy* and *Gammer Gurton's Needle*. I saw one *Hamlet* performed on the walls of New College, and another, with an actual Dane in the main role, performed in the Town Hall. At the time, I was possessed by *Hamlet*, imagining myself half-mad. Which I was.

There were Restoration romps by Wycherley, Congreve and Vanbrugh, the latter's *The Relapse* being an especial delight. Of course there was plenty of Shakespeare and Marlowe, with a particularly memorable *Edward II* played in Oriel quad in freezing summer weather, with Neville Siggs as the King. Darkness fell as we sat watching the improvised stage.

The black Jacobean plays of Webster and Tourneur particularly attracted me, with their sense of guilt, revenge motifs and flashes of poetry. Webster, of course, was much possessed by death, and saw the skull beneath the skin, as T. S. Eliot

noted. Both Webster and Tourneur remain mysterious figures, about whom little is known; yet their savage entertain-
ments have survived over three and a half centuries. Only
recently, we saw a striking new production of *The Revenger's
Tragedy* at Stratford. *The Atheist's Tragedy* contains some fine
poetry, though it is rarely performed.

Undergraduate companies had limited resources. One
courtier and a curtain were made to stand for the riches of a
Renaissance court, while the bad barons of English history
padded out their stature with common-room cushions and an
extra pair of rugger socks.

Ben Jonson's marvellously funny *Epicene, or the Silent Woman*
was played in Mansfield College gardens, produced by Frank
Hauser, later director of the Meadow Players at the Oxford
Playhouse. In the cast were such future celebrities as Robert
Hardy, Norman Painting (who, after graduating, went into
The Archers), Daphne Levens and John Schlesinger. Jonson's
plays, stodgy to read, come alive on the stage. *Epicene* was an
OUDS production. The OU Experimental Theatre Club put
on a stunning *Troilus and Cressida*, the cast including Russell
Enoch (later the William Russell of TV's *Robin Hood* fame),
Michael Croft and Paul Vaughan — not forgetting a black-clad
Ulysses, the future Chairman of British Rail, Peter Parker.

This *Troilus* was performed in the grounds of Halifax
House. The night I attended, Ken Tynan and Alan Brien
were in the audience, the two great rivals in wit who filled the
middle pages of *Isis* magazine, Tynan on theatre on one side,
Brien on films on the other.

The Playhouse – closed in 1989 — boasted a good repertory
company in my early days in Oxford. On Monday nights,
seats were half-price. I remember in particular a terrific production of Sheridan's funniest comedy, *The Critic*, the cast
including such regular stalwarts as John McKelvey, Jack
Cassidy and John Moffatt, so good in Restoration comedy.

Those were years of revelation for me. Every day brought
new discoveries. I fell into books in my eagerness to catch up

on all those years lost in the sun. History, philosophy, psychology, biography, literature, art: the bookshop became my library. When Sanders promoted me to buyer of new books, I ordered from publishers whatever interested me. I believed that if I filled the shop with books I liked I would have no difficulty in selling them. It was intoxicating to stock up with any book I wanted. Sanders must have been crazy to give me my head as he did.

Many writers I have loved since that time, among them Lewis Mumford, Benjamin Robert Haydon (I was directed to him by Aldous Huxley), Logan Pearsall Smith, Kafka – on, the list goes on – and two poets who were at that time Oxford favourites, John Donne and T. S. Eliot. Donne and Eliot have proved of lasting interest, poets who can always be turned to. And there were others, some of whom have failed to gain universal approval, like Roy Campbell. A line or two of Roy Campbell went into *Helliconia Spring*, just as Tourneur went into *Eighty-Minute Hour*.

There was much to please. And a dilemma. Reality consisted of several conflicting *umwelts* partially overlapping. It might be codified like this:

I was in the top box. How was I to gain possession of all four boxes?

A frantic division of energies filled those few hours when I was free of Sanders. Food, women and writing were in competition. In the room at 13 King Edward Street, I generally worked on worthless poems and verse plays under the one central light. I had several girlfriends, most of them as poor as I, most of them content with a visit to the cinema and an hour or two in a snug waste-paper house accessible at the end of Sanders' side passage, to which fortunately I had a key.

The need for food was pressing. When I arrived in Oxford, several British Restaurants were in existence. They disappeared one by one as their task of catering to a wartime workforce was fulfilled. One restaurant stood on an old coal wharf by the canal which was later filled in to become part of the ground on which Nuffield College now stands.

The British Restaurant in the Town Hall was always well attended. Queues sometimes stretched down the imposing staircase to the entrance doors and beyond, into St Aldate's, but they moved quickly. Many students ate there. It was a good place to pick up girls. Everyone was friendly in a sort of post-war way, and the ladies who served there knew their regulars. A three-course meal cost 1s. 3d. (pronounced one-and-three, or seven pence by present currency).

What was the main course? Sometimes it was Vienna Steak. We have all adapted to change. Even what goes into our stomachs has changed. Today, the Vienna Steak is extinct. The term was a euphemism for rissole. It came with thick gravy and mashed potato and an unheard Strauss waltz. As night gives way to day, so the Vienna Steak gave way to the Hamburger.

And the question I asked myself was, whether I was stuck for ever in Sanders' shop with the taste of Vienna Steak in my mouth. There was no one to rescue me, unless I could make those marks on paper make sense.

Those restaurants were very utilitarian, more like *1984* than

37

one cared to mention. When Indian restaurants opened in England, they were thrice welcome. They did not make you ashamed of frayed cuffs, assuming from the start that you were poor and needed something peppy under your belt. When I first saw Indians and Chinese in Oxford, I followed them down the street, for the mere pleasure of the sight of them among all the pale Caucasian faces.

So I wrote. At one of the first Faber parties I went to, I met John Bowen, now a big name in television. Bowen is a clever writer with a flair for fantasy; an early novel of his, *After the Rain*, was a successful science fiction novel. But he warned me at that party that there was no money to be made in writing SF. I remember his words: "You don't want to have a bottle of Heinz salad cream on your table all your life, do you?"

Often when I pour walnut oil or lemon on my salad, I think of Bowen – and that naughty, corrupting question of his.

CHAPTER 4

Imaginary Diaries

Here is how my first book came into being. A publisher stepped forward and asked me to write it. I never papered my room in King Edward Street with rejection slips. I don't know what a rejection slip looks like. No wonder I have been so difficult ever since.

Always have a change of scene with a new chapter. So here is another bookshop: Parker's of Oxford. Sanders has fallen away underfoot. Parker's paid fair wages and let its staff go at five thirty. I gained ten extra hours of liberty per week. Parker's closed down in 1988, to make way for Blackwell's art shop.

I called a halt to poetry writing, and launched into short stories. Using the extra free time as an investment, I began to write a novel entitled "Shouting Down a Cliff".

"Shouting Down a Cliff" took up two summers and all the time in between. It was written in two large hard-covered notebooks, in longhand, with one of those fountain pens containing a little rubber tube to hold the ink, predecessor of today's cartridge pen. What rendered those pens obsolete was the dawn of cheap air travel in the sixties. At 30,000 feet, the old rubber-interior pens, under change in air pressure, would discharge their contents into one's pocket.

If "Shouting Down a Cliff" is not a title which springs to

mind as readily as, say, *David Copperfield* or *Lord of the Flies*, this is because it has never been published. I never even typed it out from the notebooks. It was never offered to a publisher. I was convinced before it was finished that it was scarcely up to scratch. A critical faculty is not the least of a writer's gifts.

Where "Shouting Down a Cliff" differs from the novels of many other unpublished novelists working at that time in Oxford – everyone seemed to be at it – is that I finished it. It was complete. Eighty thousand words. Finito. I had seen it through.

If I had written a novel I could do anything.

"Shouting" was about ordinary life, which held profound mysteries for me, and still does. I was reading Proust's novel, with its astonishing *aperçus*, and, at the same time, devouring the science fiction magazines which abounded in the fifties, before the paperback revolution. After years of being exclusively faithful to *Astounding*, I was turning to *Galaxy*, *The Magazine of Fantasy & Science Fiction* and *If*. Other magazines surfaced occasionally, *Thrilling Wonder* and *Dynamic* being my favourites. At this period I knew nobody else who read science fiction. For that matter, I knew nobody else who was reading Proust.

In 1955, a considerable Proust exhibition was mounted in the Wildenstein Gallery in London. Of course I had the common ambition to imitate Proust, except that my terrific long novel would have scenes on Mars and the moons of Jupiter. It would be splendid and unprecedented. I went to the exhibition.

The chief exhibit, displayed in long glass cases, was *les cahiers*, the final manuscript of *A la recherche du temps perdu*, all written in many exercise books. In the Master's spidery hand.

Never again did I write in longhand. This century certainly has its advantages, among which must be numbered the electronic typewriter, on which I am writing the first draft of this book, and the word-processor. Think not only of Marcel Proust but of poor Countess Tolstoi, who copied out *War and*

Peace five times in longhand for her husband. In Cyrillic, too. No wonder their marriage was so awful. Take advantage of what technology has to offer.

I bought a typewriter and became more professional. These days I also have a fax machine.

Parker's in my time was L-shaped. I worked in the Turl end with Don Chaundy. Whenever the door opened about lunch-time, we could smell the curry from the Taj Mahal restaurant opposite.

The weekly journal of the book trade is, and was then, *The Bookseller*. Every week it filtered down the long vertical of the L and round the foot of the L to Chaundy and me. It got to us fairly speedily, because few of the staff bothered to read it.

(God, I yawn to think of those days. Why aren't I in New York, where the elevators sail upwards so fast and upwards is so much higher than elsewhere? Good old Manhattan, so different from Oxford . . .)

Anyhow, *The Bookseller* ran a series of articles which supposedly covered every aspect of bookshop life, although there was nothing about actually working in a shop. I wrote to the editor, Edmond Segrave, explaining that the pale face of the assistant was the backbone of literary life, and so on.

He wrote back inviting me to do an article for him. I did so in February 1954. It was so long that Segrave spread it over two issues. What a sensation! A bloody assistant having the cheek to string a few sentences together! Dark looks were cast at me in the trade.

At this point, I grasped one of the essential points of fiction, that Pretence is needed as a bodyguard for poor ailing Truth. I wrote again to Mr Segrave, saying that the only way to present the reality of the bookselling experience was to dress it as fiction. I was prepared to write him an imaginary diary – to be entitled "The Brightfount Diaries" – in six episodes, to be run in six successive issues, in order to put across what I meant.

Much is owed to Mr Segrave. He summoned me to his

offices in Bedford Square. He and his assistant, Miss Philothea Thompson, later to become editor, took me out to lunch. They agreed to run the "Diaries", although *The Bookseller* in its long history had never before published fiction.

Soon everyone in the book trade was reading and chuckling over "The Brightfount Diaries".

You see, reader, that that chapter on Sanders was not there just for padding or nostalgia, as you suspected. It was research material. Sanders was the model for Brightfount's. I just made it funnier and changed the names of the guilty parties.

"Brightfount" became so popular that Mr Segrave kept me at it. He paid me, too. I met him once more, after his retirement, in a cheerful pub called The Little Mayfair, behind the London Hilton, and we had a drink together.

While "Brightfount" was in full spate, Mr Segrave forwarded fan letters to me, from booksellers and so on, at home and overseas. The Beck Book Company wrote from Adelaide, offering me a job. I had always wanted to visit Australia. At that time, prospects sounded good out there, while the UK economy was dying on its feet as usual. Letters were exchanged. I was preparing to go when a further letter revealed what Mr Beck had until then had the cunning to keep from me, that they wanted me to run the theology department. I stayed in Oxford.

Many years later, my eyes beheld the solid brick-built glory of the Beck Book Company *in situ*. I reflected then, in a science-fictional way, on the parting of time-streams, and of the other Aldiss who nearly fled to Oz and took holy orders. That poor little pom never became a famous writer. But he was great on a surfboard.

The next letter forwarded from *The Bookseller* changed my life. It came from the firm then considered the most elegant in London, Faber & Faber, publishers of T. S. Eliot. It said that Sir Geoffrey Faber and his staff were great fans of "Brightfount", and were wondering if I had considered turning the

Diaries into a book. If so, Faber would take great pleasure in publishing it.

I still have the letter. It is on loan, with my other manuscripts, to the Bodleian Library in Oxford.

The first question readers ask writers is, What sort of routine do you have?

The second is, How did you begin to write?

To these questions – and others, such as, How do you discipline yourself? – there are various answers, depending on the writer and the time of day. Mostly readers hope to be astonished: You mean to say you write only in leap years? Routine is a hateful word. I'm a failed Bohemian, and write when and if I can. Which is most days.

I cannot remember when I was not making books. At my mother's knee I was encouraged to collect pictures from magazines, to give them captions and bind them up with pieces of wallpaper for covers.

This aided my pictorial sense. Also helpful was the family's Hobbies fretwork machine. On this machine, Mother made jigsaws from pictures stuck on to three-ply, simple jigsaws at first, then of increasing difficulty as my sister and I grew up.

My mother read to me before I could read. One of the first stories I ever read myself was in the old *Daily Mail*. A girl who lost her shadow had to travel round the world to find it. The theme touched me so closely that I coloured the illustration. Mother preserved the picture, and somehow it has survived the years.

At the tender age of seven, I was sent away to boarding school. In the junior dormitory, with its hurly-burly, I found a way of preserving my identity. I told stories.

All new boys had to tell stories. They were made to stand up on their beds and spout. If the story did not please, or the storyteller faltered, shoes were thrown at him. I never had a shoe lifted against me.

Soon I became champion storyteller. There was just one

snag: talking was forbidden after Lights Out. The house-master, Bonzo, had a spyhole by the door. He would rush in, cane in hand, switching on all the lights at once.

"Who's talking?"

Reluctantly, I would raise my hand.

The punishment was six strokes on the bum, laid on with vigour across the pyjamas. I have never met with quite that kind of criticism since, though in the comments of many critics one hears a nasty little housemaster longing to get loose.

That dormitory ritual of narrative. It was impossible to stamp out, so valuable was it. It warded off homesickness and night fears. Something very primitive was evoked when telling stories to a silent dorm.

My stories were of a lurid variety. Many of them were SF. I derived them from Murray Roberts's stories of Captain Justice, which ran in a thirties magazine, *Modern Boy*. And I did all the voices. Justice, Midge, O'Reilly and Professor Flaznagel.

Later, at a better school, West Buckland in North Devon, I graduated, or perhaps declined, from verbal to written stories. They became more ambitious, less derivative. Our form was mad about Sellers & Yeatman – not just *1066 and All That*, but the less popular titles such as *Horse Nonsense* and *Garden Rubbish*. I wrote my own version, "Invalids and Illnesses", which was popular. But my great success was with a series of pornographic stories told in Americanese. Each title came with a one-sentence blurb, in the manner of American pulp magazine stories of the forties. The titles of those stories have gone from my head; only two of the blurbs remain: "They went to New York for a change of obscenery", and "The editor's incision was final" (he died "on the job", as it was then called).

These stories brought me into even greater danger than the oral tales. Had they been discovered in one of the periodical raids carried out on our desks, I should have been beaten and expelled. But the writing madness was in my veins. I also wrote comic stories and SF stories, which I collected into books. These earned me the exemption from school essays I have described.

This experience, valuable as it was in confirming that people might listen, was interrupted by war service. For four years I was out of England, four formative years from eighteen till almost twenty-two, a not uncommon experience for my generation. Out of England and out of the class system and the stream of English thought. I left the country a mere boy and returned as an adult. In those years, 1944-48, England also had changed. Pre-war England had gone for ever.

Nowadays, the trauma of being involved in war, or in any kind of catastrophe – a rail accident, say – is better understood than it was. We understand how necessary it may be to talk through a trying experience, just as young lovers whisper to their partners all the shortcomings of their parents. Confession is the way to mental stability.

In Burma, stuck in the jungle with Japanese forces only a few miles away, the older men spoke fiercely of how they would "grip" their audiences when they returned home, relating their sufferings. Like the Ancient Mariner, they intended to tell all: in the hope of release from trauma, which was also the Ancient Mariner's ambition. Just as the wedding guest tried to evade the long and tiresome story, I'm sure all of us in the "Forgotten Army" in Burma found our friends at home, when we returned, just as reluctant to listen. We may also have discovered that some experiences could hardly attain speech.

For some years, when I was reinstated in that baffling place, England, I had nightmares in which the Japanese were advancing on me with bayonets fixed. Writing was a form of exorcism.

During demobilisation leave, I sat down to write my first novel. It was to be called "Hunter Leaves the Herd" and would tell England what the Far East was like. It was about a deserter from the army. It never got written. I had not the

45

equipment at the time to write a whole novel.

I took my typewriter and went up to Oxford to get a job. When interviewing me, Mr Sanders said, "Which contemporary novelist is your favourite?"

I do not know why I did not say Aldous Huxley or Evelyn Waugh (who had not then gone off the gold standard with *Brideshead Revisited*). I said "Eric Linklater", as being more down to earth.

Later, Sanders said to me, "You know, I'd never heard of Linklater."

But Linklater, with his bawdy sense of humour and jaunty narrative, was for many years a great favourite. I collected all his novels, plays and stories; they left my shelves only when my old home broke up.

After "The Hunter Leaves the Herd" died on the vine, I wrote nothing but poetry, most of it inspired by the girls I met in Oxford. Then came "Shouting Down a Cliff".

While on holiday in the Isle of Wight, I bought from a newsagent an SF magazine called *Nebula*, published in Glasgow, and read it on the beach. The stories were so amateur I knew I could do better, though I admired one by Bob Shaw. I had an acceptance from Peter Hamilton, the editor. It took him over three years to publish the story: called simply "T" – it remains my shortest title – it was finished on 30 January 1953. I received Hamilton's cheque in January 1955, and the story was published in November 1956. (One keeps such details of early stories; later stories are less slavishly documented.) By the end of November 1956 my career was launched. My first book had been published by Faber & Faber and a second one was in the works.

I needed to see inferior writing in order to encourage myself that I could do better. I knew no one, took no advice. To work in a bookshop is to know a world already full of books.

The title of my second book was *Space, Time and Nathaniel*. It was a collection of SF short stories. The title was distinctive, announcing the fact that I did not intend to follow a trail worn by other British SF writers. None of them wrote well enough, to my mind, except J. G. Ballard, another "discovery" of Carnell's.

A firmly entrenched belief in the book trade is that collections of short stories do not sell. On average, they sell less well than novels, and novels on average sell poorly enough. Publishing is a hard trade. But *Space, Time and Nathaniel* is still in print, thirty years on, having lived through four different English imprints. American publishers could not stand the silly title, and eventually issued an emasculated version under a generic – and therefore flavourless – title, *No Time Like Tomorrow*. Exactly the sort of thing that makes one hate being an SF writer. Spanish, German and French editions also appeared, the French Denoël edition being translated by Michel Deutsch, my first and possibly happiest French translator.

What was there in that volume which moved Kenneth Young, reviewing the collection in *The Daily Telegraph*, to claim that the stories conveyed "a true sense of wonder such as we find in Blake or Wordsworth"? The answer must be that their author was delighted with the majesty of the world, the possibilities in science fiction and the freedom of imagination which writing brought him.

CHAPTER 5

Elegy for Minor Poets

The choice of publisher looms as a large decision in every writer's life. As with many other things, advice is not much use.

If you have friends in publishing, the choice is made for you. You go to them, hoping the friendship will hold up. For most people, however, it is more a matter of *sauve qui peut*. You go to whoever is mad enough to accept your manuscript.

Not all publishers are alike, though all bear family resemblances. Authors can join the Society of Authors, which lives at 84 Drayton Gardens, in London, and the Society will advise. I am a member of the Council of the Society of Authors and an active member of the Writers' Guild of Great Britain.

Although publishers are necessary, it is as well to remember that what you write is more important than which publisher publishes it – and what you write is fully within your own powers of decision. It's useless to be a writer unless you enjoy the freedom and responsibility to decide.

How long has it taken you to read this far? Let me tell you how long it has taken to write this far. It is now the twenty-seventh of September, 1985, at four thirty of a golden afternoon. The chair, the table, the typewriter, I – all outside my study on the lawn. I am thinking of breaking off for a mug of tea, a little conversation and a walk round the garden. Then an hour or two more work. I have to go to a play-reading this evening.

I have worked on this typescript all afternoon. This morning I answered letters. I am also working on two or three other books.

There's a novel called "Whitehall", which is tentative and may never get itself finished. Whitehall was the name of my grandfather's house. There is the massive revision of my history of science fiction, *Trillion Year Spree*, which I am undertaking with the assistance of David Wingrove. And there is, or may be at any moment, depending on how the cards fall, "The Helliconia Encyclopaedia", which has hovered over David and me, appearing and disappearing like the grin of the Cheshire cat, for two or three years.

This is a day of pure, still autumn, with butterflies exploring cactus dahlias and nasturtiums, creative weather. After a difficult year, when I have struggled to get near a typewriter, creative juices flow again. I began writing part of this narrative yesterday, at nine o'clock, moved by the beauty of the evening. I saw the whole book clear: something which might help aspiring writers and perhaps amuse all my comrades-in-arms, the great reviewed.

The family went to bed as I tapped away. I sat in a pool of electric light in my study while moonlight poured in through the window. Jackson, one of our dearest cats, arrived and scratched at the window to be let in. He has taught me a few simple gestures like that. When he was in, Jackson settled down on a chair. But I climbed out of the window and walked in the garden. All was silent. A full moon loomed over the pines in a stagy way, recalling Böcklin's *The Isle of the Dead*. A quick rejoice and then back to the typewriter.

It is easy to become a writer. Easy, that is, compared with remaining a writer. To remain a writer you have to continue to write. If you take a year off, it is hard to get back in the flow. Better, and ultimately more enjoyable, to fall into the habit of writing every day. If you have to go on a train journey, talk to the others in the carriage; make notes of what you see, of what they say. If you feel like it.

Too early success in writing may quench a desire to write more. So may too early failure. So for that matter may a lot of other things. Many things can go wrong in the happiest of careers, and little charity is extended to those who fall by the wayside.

Louis MacNeice's "Elegy for Minor Poets" celebrates those for whom writing did not bring success:

> Who were lost in many ways, through comfort,
>   lack of knowledge,
> Or between women's breasts, who thought
>   too little, too much,
> Who were the world's best talkers, in tone and
>   rhythm
> Superb, yet as writers lacked a sense of touch,
> So either gave up or just went on and on –
> Let us salute them now their chance is gone.

Long-sustained creativity over a number of years involves two overlapping parts of the personality, the intellect and the emotions.

The intellect seeks to make sense, or at least a pattern, out of the universe with which it is confronted. We may consider that in the ordinary person this seeking holds no great urgency, except perhaps in adolescence; it may be satisfied by a religion or an ideology of some kind, which lends a framework to daily life. Even the weekly football pool may make a kind of pattern to life; behind it lies a wish, not only to win money, but to control – on however small a scale – future events.

The search for a pattern may be painfully intensified in those whose upbringing, for whatever reason, was disturbed. In its extreme form, this disturbance may lead to a paranoid personality, who sees his or her world in terms of a conspiracy against him (it is usually a him). Painful this may be, but at least the intellect has its pattern. Something is satisfied.

Writers, so it seems, live somewhere between these two extremes. They feel the need to search, to seek for a pattern. Their books may represent separate, almost unrelated attempts to find this pattern; each book is a transient pattern in itself. Other writers, perhaps the more important ones, seek more comprehensive orders; their writings will be all related. Critics then speak confidently of such a writer's development. Our leading writers, Graham Greene, Iris Murdoch and Doris Lessing, are accorded such attention.

This is not to say that such authors verge on paranoia, although Graham Greene has declared that he would have become a criminal if he had not turned writer. It is to say that, in this respect, they are not ordinary people; and their profession slowly separates them from the ordinariness they once possessed. (Of course, in every other respect they may be perfectly ordinary, shop in Marks & Spencer, weed the garden, travel on the Northern Line.)

"The human mind seems to be so constructed that the discovery, or perception, of order or unity in the external world is mirrored, transferred, and experienced as if it were a discovery of a new order and balance in the inner world of the psyche." So says Anthony Storr, who has written more clearly about creativity than anyone. The quotation comes from his book, *The School of Genius*.

When I was seven, I had need to cling on to something. I had at the time a microscope, a telescope and a small kaleidoscope. These instruments were my toys. I drew what I saw down the microscope, I studied the stars and moon, I watched the shifting patterns of colour in the kaleidoscope. These toys directed my attention, at a critical phase of my development, outwards. My interest as a science fiction writer has been to make sense of the universe, to express the order I found there, and to relate that order – as Storr says – to the inner world of the psyche.

The universe is a dynamic place these days, not at all the simple clockwork machine it was depicted as being during the nineteen-thirties. New discoveries crowd in on us all the while. The same holds good for our inner world. We may establish a pattern which, to our satisfaction, corresponds with events "out there"; but nothing stays put and, in a while, we may feel the urge to attempt the equation again. Of course, if our vision extends no further than the gatepost, we may never be troubled in this way.

And what of readers? Reading is a creative occupation — much more so than watching television. A reader conspires with an author; they are two people rapt in a singular sort of communion; a writer's work is not complete without his readers. He may not need many, or he may need multitudes; but he (or she) has to fight somehow to get in touch with the right audience. I believe that readers, people who are continually reading books, are very similar to writers; they may lack a degree of creativity, but they also seek to make sense, or a pattern, out of the universe with which they are presented.

Anthony Storr puts this well in his work, *The Dynamics of Creation*, when he says, "By identifying ourselves, however fleetingly, with the creator, we can participate in the integrating process which he has carried out for himself." We all seek an identity; for writers as for actors this is often a primary concern. As Seurat's paintings were formed from a multitude of coloured dots, so our identity gradually crystallises from our own view of the universe, or personal *umwelt*.

Long-sustained creativity involves more than the intellect. The emotions are also brought into play.

I have mentioned instruments I valued as a boy, telescopes, microscopes and kaleidoscopes. These are scientific instruments, but there are two sorts of science, the science which observes nature and the science which attempts to alter nature (Victor Frankenstein was the first scientist of the latter kind). I was, even at the age of seven, of the passive kind. I observed.

For better or worse, this is one key to character. There is some evidence that writers are happier in the role of observer.

Writing, like the other arts, entails many hours of labour, often in solitary state. If measured on a conventional scale of payment, the financial returns for these hours of labour are in general nugatory. Why then these hours of labour? One answer must be that they represent a defence against the outside world.

Creativity is generally a mystery, even to the creative person himself. The popular view of creativity follows the "pearl in the oyster" theory, which, in a slapdash way, embodies truth. The conception of Beethoven composing his symphonies despite his deafness, or Goya painting on despite a similar affliction, has a romantic appeal. The slavery of creative work may seem like a freedom if it protects the creator from worse things, from some loss in childhood, from a fear of the terrible vacuum.

Anthony Storr, the authority on creativity, says:

> If creative work protects a man against mental illness, it is small wonder that he pursues it with avidity; and even if the state of mind he is seeking to avoid is no more than a mild state of depression or apathy, this still constitutes a cogent reason for engaging in creative work even when it brings no obvious external benefit in its train.

It would appear that writing in the present day is a preserve best suited to the rather withdrawn personality, who is able to endure and even enjoy solitude. And not only in the present day. Vasari, writing his *Lives of the Painters* in the sixteenth century, claims that love of his art makes a man solitary and meditative, saying it is necessary that "he who takes up the study of art should flee the company of men". Seclusion is an inseparable part of the pattern of intellectual and spiritual life in East and West alike.

In sum, there are intellectual and emotional patterns which

have proved over the years to be peculiar to creative people. If you are a star footballer and you feel the impulse to write a book, the chance is that you will write only one. To be a real writer over a number of years, you must have stamina and the right psychological make-up.

Many think that the writer's life is an enviable one. I am certainly of that number. But it has its shadowed side. A wish to unburden oneself is, after all, an indication that one is burdened. So it proves, according to recent researches on both sides of the Atlantic.

Poets are well known to be prone to phases of depression. Their numbers include William Cowper – a poet in whom I once took personal interest, being born in the town where he died – Tennyson, Coleridge, John Donne, John Berryman, Louis MacNeice, Thomas Hardy, Christopher Smart, John Clare (who spent many years in a madhouse), Gerard Manley Hopkins, Anne Sexton, Hart Crane, Randall Jarrell, Sylvia Plath, Robert Lowell, and others. Crane, Berryman, Jarrell, Sexton and Plath committed suicide, Cowper attempted it.

Several of these writers suffered bereavements early in life. Cowper lost his mother when he was four, and cannot be said ever to have recovered from the loss. The melancholy A. E. Housman's mother died on his twelfth birthday.

Coleridge, Edgar Allan Poe, Berryman, MacNeice and Plath all lost a parent before the age of twelve. The author of *Frankenstein* lost her mother when she was born, and her novel is heavy with that loss.

A group of writers investigated at a writers' workshop at the University of Iowa in 1974 showed that, of fifteen authors, nine had seen a psychiatrist, eight had been treated with drugs or by psychotherapy, and four had been admitted to hospital. Six had symptoms of alcoholism, and one committed suicide later.

In February 1986, the *Sunday Times* published the results of research into forty-seven of Britain's leading writers by Dr Kay Jamison of the University of California in Los Angeles.

Ten of the eighteen poets who responded had received treatment for psychological disorders, while half of them had been treated for mania with strong anti-depressant drugs such as lithium, and had voluntarily undergone electro-convulsive therapy or spent time in hospital.

Two of the eight novelists who responded to the survey had been mentally ill. As A. Alvarez says in his study of suicide, *The Savage God*, "The better the artist, the more vulnerable he seems to be."

Of course, it is not the writing which causes the depression, but rather the depressed who choose writing. And, it must be added, the term "depressed personality" is used here in a clinical way. Those who are depressed in the common-or-garden sense of that term are probably incapable of looking constructively at a considerable body of work such as a novel or play.

The clinically depressed are often remarkably cheerful. That may be the face they choose to present to the world.

Or, or course, they may just have had a book accepted by Faber & Faber.

CHAPTER 6

Recuperation: a Brief Chapter

The Brightfount Diaries was published by Faber & Faber on 2 November 1955.

Parker's loyally ordered a half-dozen copies on sale or return. Their faith in their staff was rewarded. The copies sold out by lunchtime. I was safe round the other end of the shop, hiding behind piles of second-hand books; but I had had my hair cut for the occasion.

Along came the reporter from the Local Paper. He proved to be as embarrassed as I was. He took a few notes, brushing back a lock of hair from his forehead as he did so. It immediately fell back again. Later, I had a few drinks with him. He was a poet. His name was Adrian Mitchell. His first novel, *If You See Me Comin'*, was published while he was working on the *Oxford Mail*.

Parker's, meanwhile, ordered two hundred and fifty copies of *Brightfount*. A poster was produced with a photograph of me in the shop. A whole window was filled with my pink-jacketed book. Over in Blackwell's, they became pretty suspicious of me.

Then the reviews began to come in. Suppose the reviewers did not find the book amusing, I thought to myself. Well, if they don't enjoy the thing, I never have to write another. It was a weasel thought. I would like to think I never thought it.

56

Fortunately, the reviewers took a lenient view.

Years like 1955 are few and far between. There were the *Observer* short story prize for "Not For an Age", early short stories published, *Brightfount* a success, and my first child, Clive, born. A thrilling hope filled me. Perhaps I might redeem the wasted years and prove myself of some worth. It was never making money which interested me, but making good.

After *Brightfount*, Faber went on to publish my science fiction. I was fortunate to be with the one publisher in London at that time where people liked and understood science fiction. Sir Geoffrey Faber and his daughter Ann and fellow-director Charles Monteith all read it. Charles had just had his great success in discovering William Golding and *Lord of the Flies*, a novel he rescued from the slush pile. Both Charles and Golding were SF readers. Charles, who became my editor, was ever generous, hospitable and amusing. He had fought in Burma, and was wounded in the Arakan, generally reckoned to be the nastiest sector of the Burma theatre.

Faber parties were rather alarming. The company was then housed at 24 Russell Square, on a corner. With what awe one approached the building. The Faber list was a comprehensive one, beginning with literature and moving through Hugh Ross Williamson and David Stacton to science fiction, nursing and gardening. Those guests who wisely feared to join the incense-burners grouped round John Lehmann – such men as Cyril Connolly, W. H. Auden, Professor Trypannis, and other sweet singers – could easily find themselves entangled in discussions concerning mastectomy and hydrangeas. Daniel George, a celebrated littérateur of his day, was kind and amusing, treating the event like a day at the races, naming, with annotations, each celebrity as he or she entered. "There goes Colin Wilson. You can tell he slept on Hampstead Heath last night. And that's Alfred Duggan, who never sleeps . . . "

One could be spoken to by T. S. Eliot at Faber parties. He had his office near Charles's. I was taken to meet him in his room containing the famous pencil portraits by Wyndham

Lewis of Eliot and Pound. Eliot had the look of a rather shabby eagle. He was polite and talked of the paperclip over-population problem. This was Eliot being the publisher; he was not in his poet persona.

It was pleasant to be treated as a writer, but there remained the nagging question, Was one actually a writer? Only when four or five books had accumulated on the shelf did it seem that something stood between me and mortality. Many more years had to pass before I woke one morning and realised that I was – inextricably, irremediably, incurably – a Writer. And no one could take that away from me; I had that greatest of securities, a life's work, and could afford to play other than safe in various ways.

There is the brute necessity of earning a living. Some writers, highly praised, gain little financial reward. The great James Joyce industry came too late to aid the living Joyce – penury in Zurich and all that. Some writers, highly praised, enjoy massive financial reward: Anthony Burgess, I'm happy to see, is classed as a millionaire. Yet there are writers who receive no critical laurels – the sort who are never reviewed in the *TLS* or the literary weeklies – but are several times richer than Burgess. Some writers who gather no critical praise reap no financial reward either. And there are authors like Graham Greene who seem to have everything.

LESSON ONE: Financial reward is no criterion of an author's merit.

LESSON TWO: Financial failure is no criterion of an author's merit.

In the past, I have felt pressure on me to write a book a year. That is, a novel, a collection of short stories, or a non-fiction book. This year, 1989, I happen to be writing three books, though not all may pass the winning post of completion.

Behind me lies a year where I wrote nothing fruitful, unless a thousand letters are fruitful, which I doubt.

As to why I wrote nothing. Over the seven previous years, I wrote the three long Helliconia novels, a total of almost half a million words. Into those novels, I tried to pour all that I knew, of writing and of the world. My endeavour was to encompass all my experience. After that, the ground had to lie fallow.

CHAPTER 7

In the Big Spaceship

W. H. Smith's used to be one of my stamping grounds when I was first in Oxford. It was an excellent shop, the manager being a small, nervous man called Kessel. We got to know each other and he once offered me a job. Perhaps I should have taken it. I could have been a manager by now . . .

A difficulty was that I did not see myself as one of a large staff. In the army, I had been one of a large staff for four and a half years.

Smith's in those days ran a lending library, and sold its rejects on a bench outside the shop. The library went long ago. Nowadays the books are all tucked away upstairs. Other booksellers like Tim Waterstone have come along, who hold more evangelical attitudes towards books, and now Waterstone has been bought by Smith's.

But it was outside Smith's of Cornmarket, Oxford, that I bought for one shilling an *ex-libris* copy of George R. Stewart's *Earth Abides*. Its vision moved me towards a holistic and ecological approach to writing. It was necessary to shed the influence of P. G. Wodehouse.

Some time or other, we have to tack our colours to the mast. Otherwise, goodbye, mast!

I was in Faber's offices after *Brightfount* was published, talking to Charles Monteith and Geoffrey Faber.

"The book's doing well," they said. "What are you going to write next?"

"I also," I said, "write science fiction."

To have a career in writing – well, I hardly see what the phrase means, unless it means to be not so much a writer as a careerist, with, as an ultimate objective, perhaps a hotel in the Bahamas, or an estate in Tuscany – retiring from writing, in other words, rather than actually *becoming a writer*.

Ian Fleming made writing his career, and was eminently successful in it. His strategy was a time-honoured one, still recommended to those who wish to make money. Fleming invented a hero with whom many could comfortably identify, and related his adventures in a series of easily readable novels (no easy task, as imitators have discovered). The adventures took on a formulaic, almost heraldic, pattern, from which Fleming did not depart. James Bond did not age. The closer Fleming kept to the established pattern, working minor variations within the pattern, the more he pleased his readers. Fleming roused and then fulfilled generic expectations, as Agatha Christie had done.

These matters are clearly understood. It is useless to be too clever. We cannot have Hercule Poirot throwing up his hands in Chapter Thirty-three, declaring that he is baffled, and retiring to Belgium. Dr No cannot actually remove James Bond's threatened testicles. That's a no-no. The cleverness of Ian Fleming was in not being too clever: he fulfilled generic expectations.

It is easy to understand the success of James Bond after the event. On the whole, the mass of people share Bond's tastes. Expensive cars, pretty girls, adventure, drink. All the world loves a dry martini. But to deliver with Fleming's style – that's another matter.

In 1955, the Fleming craze was in its infancy; but the general principles of his later success were already accepted. Tarzan, Bulldog Drummond, The Saint and other formula heroes had been there before him. If at the outset of one's writing life one decided to make a lot of money, one could follow that trail. Not only did it seem profitable, thrillers were also respectable. Dons read them, horsy people in country houses read them, clergy read them.

If at the outset of one's writing life one decided to fail at literature, science fiction was a good bet. No one read it. Not knowingly.

The British have the best science fiction writers in the world. All the ignorance of critics cannot make it otherwise. Mary Shelley, H. G. Wells, Olaf Stapledon, E. M. Forster, G. K. Chesterton, Aldous Huxley, George Orwell, J. R. R. Tolkien, Kingsley Amis, Martin Amis, Adrian Mitchell, Angela Carter, Doris Lessing, Anthony Burgess have all written science fiction or something very like it. Yet the mode remains largely ignored by critics brought up only to appreciate the novel of character.

Commercial science fiction, branded as such, had, in 1955, only just escaped from a shuttle service of magazines, mainly American. Some regular hardcover American publishers had taken it on to their lists. In consequence, British publishers, making their annual raid on the fleshpots of New York, had returned with a token handful of this mysterious new literature which their US counterparts, barely concealing their mirth, had assured them would sell like crazy.

William Heinemann, for instance, began a science fiction list, labelled as such, put out with memorably awful covers. Among several good titles, such as L. Sprague de Camp's *Lest Darkness Fall*, in which a twentieth-century man is cast back in time to Rome of the Dark Ages, where he must live on his wits, was a famous novel, Pohl and Kornbluth's *The Space Merchants*, a satire on the advertising industry, which sells real estate on the loathsome surface of Venus. Heinemann's was the first hardcover edition. This novel has gone through many editions since, and many translations. Yet the Heinemann edition was soon being sold off, remaindered along with the other titles.

The British reading public was not ready for such delights. Or something.

Other publishers like Weidenfeld & Nicolson and Michael Joseph had little better luck — though Joseph's series, strangely enough under the editorship of Clemence Dane, best known as a playwright, featured good indigenous authors such as John Christopher. Gollancz's SF list had not yet been launched.

Science fiction was not, in 1955, considered at all a commercial proposition. Nor did it lend prestige to any publisher who might embark on it.

So when I told Charles and Sir Geoffrey that I wrote science fiction, I was scarcely prepared for their response.

"Oh, good," they said. "Let's see it."

That first letter I had received from Faber, tremblingly opened in Parker's, had had five successors from other publishers. Each publisher, in fairly glowing terms, wrote to invite me to join their list and turn the "Brightfount" column into a book. None had been as quick off the mark as Charles Monteith. None was just starting an SF list.

Faber then published a perennial series called *My Best* – . Walter de la Mare edited *My Best Ghost Story*, for instance; I read the collection as a boy, and shivered over Oliver Onions' "The Beckoning Fair One". Charles had persuaded a friend of his from university days to edit *Best SF*. So immediately successful was this volume that the editor was prevailed upon to set to work on *Best SF Two*. (Ultimately, seven *Best SF*s appeared.)

In addition, Faber were casting about for new SF authors to grace their list. Clifford Simak was one of them, and James Blish another. I was soon to join them.

Meanwhile, I encountered the editor of *Best SF*. His name was Bruce Montgomery. He wrote detective stories under the name of Edmund Crispin, and it was under the name Crispin that he edited the SF anthologies. Under his own name, he was composing incidental music for most of the British films of the period. Bruce's love of music is reflected also in his detective stories.

We met first in the Randolph Hotel in Oxford, in 1961. Bruce drank whisky and Canadian Club. The Canadian Club impressed me because it was advertised on the back cover of *Astounding*, which we both read. There was about Bruce a certain amused fastidiousness towards most aspects of life, though not to whisky, which made him the dearest and funniest of friends. Women idolised him and pursued him; he was too indolent to pursue them – perhaps a rule to remember. He was handsome and generous, and always intended a career in "good literature" – but was too indolent to pursue that either. I admired his indolence, and enjoyed sharing in it, although it remains a quality I have never achieved for myself.

Bruce was lured some way into the SF world. He was a close friend of two other rather more combative supporters of SF, Kingsley Amis and Robert Conquest. My admiration of these two, particularly of Kingsley, was great. Both were witty. Kingsley had a substantial range of imitations of startling veracity; Boswell imitating Johnson and Garrick can have been no more impressive. Once one had seen Amis doing John Braine being sick, one's grasp of literature improved by leaps and bounds. Kingsley did a lifelike imitation of Bruce. Such parody springs from love. Bruce is still missed.

Writers constantly have a series of traps laid for them, into which, over a publisher's lunch perhaps, they are invited to fall. Grub Street beckons. "Come on down," it says. It will give you a hand. Just beware the dirty nails.

In 1955 it chanced that I found myself on one occasion climbing a wooden stair, to the treads of which linoleum had been tacked, to meet an editor of a small paperback firm called Hamilton (Stafford) Ltd. This was in the Goldhawk Road, London. It was dark and incomprehensible inside the building, with mysterious activities in progress as if, only five minutes before my arrival, the owners of the place had decided to switch from vulcanising the tyres of army vehicles to turning out garish paperbacks and girlie calendars.

The editor was genial. His office – or *landing*, as it had been five minutes earlier – was padded with the latest titles. He showed me one or two. "Menace on the Mekong", and so on.

"Why don't you write something like this for me?"

"You publish a science fiction magazine. I want to write science fiction."

"Science fiction doesn't pay. French Foreign Legion books pay. They're easy to write. Have you read *Beau Geste?*"

"Yes."

"Then you can write a French Foreign Legion story. Except that the Foreign Legion is now in Indo-China. Where were you in the war?"

"Burma. Sumatra."

"Then you can do Indo-China, no problem. Sixty thousand words, and we pay you seventy-five pounds on the nail. How about it?"

There was no chance of my embarking on this scheme. But the encounter is of interest for two reasons. Perhaps something in the mentality of the lower echelons of paperback publishers caused them to call themselves after animals which lurked in trees or frequented Welsh mountains, or both. There were Corgi Books and Squirrel Books and Badger Books and Puffins and Panthers. Hamilton (Stafford) Ltd produced Panthers. Panthers developed, as English society developed at that time, into something more complex. Later, Panther became part of Granada, now Grafton Books, part of the Collins empire. They left those linoleum-clad steps far behind to reside in Mayfair, pillars of integrity, publishers of Ludlum.

Temptation lay in the suggestion that I turn out a French Foreign Legion book. It would have given me a chance to write about the East.

The longing for foreign places – or alien planets – had survival value in evolutionary terms. It kept the tribes on the move. Nowadays, many countries depend on it: tourism is an industry: the tribes are still on the move. George Borrow – a

65

great traveller born in East Dereham, Norfolk – understood the longing well.

In his book, *Wild Wales*, Borrow reports a conversation with the landlord of an inn whom he meets staggering over the hills.

> "Ah, landlord!" said I. "Whither bound?"
>
> "To Rhivabon," said he huskily, "for a pint."
>
> "Is the ale so good at Rhivabon," said I, "that you leave home for it?"
>
> "No," said he, rather shortly, "there's not a glass of good ale in Rhivabon."
>
> "Then why do you go thither?" said I.
>
> "Because a pint of bad liquor abroad is better than a quart at home," said the landlord, reeling against the hedge.

Chapter LXII

In the fifties, my psychic energies were directed not only towards the problems of authorship but towards forgetting that I had spent some time in parts of South-East Asia, and adjusting to civilian life.

The outbreak of war in 1939 represented a geological fault in the regular strata of English life. The England of 1947 was a drab competitive world whose features I could barely recognise. The East I had delighted in; it was always fresh and strange. And, in the armed forces, there's always company. Oxford entailed isolation among a foreign tribe. An ideal situation to be in as a writer, though I did not realise it. The two subjects I deeply needed to write about were the East and the future, both of which could contain my position of isolation.

In fact what I managed to hammer out was a fiction of self-contained worlds in which the central characters, having no safe ground, advance to a slightly more secure position, if only by dint of their painfully acquiring more knowledge. If this was what I wished to enact, then plainly I was well suited to the kind of emblematic activities which a science fiction novel embraces.

The novel eventually delivered to Charles Monteith, *Non-Stop*, contained such an example of emblematic activity. The members of the Greene tribe are lost in a strange jungle. A number of them rebel and strike out into the wilds. The truth of the situation is revealed to the reader as it is to them: that they are the remnants of the population of a large colonising spaceship which left Earth for Alpha Centauri travelling at speeds which entail several generations to complete the flight. This rather totalitarian arrangement broke down at some point on the journey.

Dominated by the image of the great ruined ship in which it is incarcerated, the group must establish just whereabouts in the universe it finds itself.

All fiction is metaphor, but some metaphors are more metaphorical than others. *Non-Stop* stood, on the surface, for the way in which technology without humanitarian concern can imprison human lives. It had an inner meaning also, involving the way in which I found my circumstances constricting and my difficulty in discerning meaning to existence. Years later, in 1975, when *Non-Stop* was published in Poland, it went to the top of the best-seller lists. Why? Because the Poles interpreted the central image as applying to their own political situation, a reading I had not visualised almost twenty years earlier.

A writer is advised to work within his limitations, and yet perhaps to defy them. Jane Austen is always held up as the writer who knew her limitations and remained within them. The Napoleonic Wars do not enter into the deliberations of the young ladies in *Pride and Prejudice*. There is no Search for Significance in Austen.

For years I was at war with myself, reading Alexander Pope and Shelley by turns. A restless personality, always set against regimentation or the restrictions of ideology, I developed my own kind of fiction, which regarded realism with disdain, while using the trappings of realism to achieve credibility. My characters are always in search of something permanent in their lives, rarely finding it. This is not untruthful.

What I longed for was someone to share my intensity. Dickens said once that all his life there was one true friend he lacked. I threw out muffled versions of myself to my readers, meat to piranhas.

It's all very well to be Jane Austen. Few achieve it. For a visionary writer, the situation is more difficult. The difficulties are increased if one is rash enough to write something categorised as "science fiction", to which an aroma of non-acceptability still clings, like muck to a farmer's boots.

Still, the visionary writer has to fly beyond what he senses. He understands that fewer readers will wish to follow him, though he himself may be sure of his course. Admittedly I was not always sure of mine. Jung, in his book on archetypes, defines the area of struggle: "Consciousness should defend its reason and protect itself, and the chaotic life of the unconscious should be given the chance of having its way too – as much of it as we can stand."

Obsessions are often deep and fruitful. It is not enough merely to have a twitch. John Wyndham had a twitch.

Nobody has yet written a life of Wyndham. It must have been a life almost beyond reproach, no attraction for a biographer. Wyndham was good-humoured, well-mannered, reserved. He produced a kind of middle-brow novel which the middle-brow English public most likes to read – except that Wyndham wrote science fiction. His remarkable gift was to lull his public into believing he did not write science fiction at all, so that they could enjoy him without qualms.

After that lunch with Ted Carnell, Carnell was as good as his word. He introduced me to John Wyndham Parkes Lucas Beynon Harris (such was his real name, and for years he had written unremarkable SF under the names of John Beynon

Harris and, later, John Beynon). At that time, *The Day of the Triffids* and *The Kraken Wakes* were famous, and *The Chrysalids*, perhaps Wyndham's best novel, was about to appear. Nothing of this could you detect from Wyndham's manner. He might have been a tea-cosy salesman for the Home Counties.

To contain the fuse of life, SF must be unsafe. Its characteristic note is insecurity. Like John Donne's love:

> It was begotten by Despair
> Upon Impossibility.

Wyndham invented the Safe SF Read.

Carnell and Wyndham and I sat in a little café in Sicilian Avenue off Southampton Row, close to Les Flood's one and only SF specialist bookshop. (Matters have improved since then with the advent of Andromeda in Birmingham and Forbidden Planet in London and New York.) Wyndham talked about his next novel. This one was not going to be so safe, by the sound of things.

Aliens were to invade Earth for a while, putting a whole English village to sleep. So far, so Wyndhamesque. While the village was asleep, the aliens were going to impregnate all the women; every woman would give birth to an alien child in nine months' time. Not so Wyndhamesque. Sex had not reared anything in his writing before.

Wyndham himself seemed unsure as to whether or not this coupling of ideas added up to a dirty joke. Carnell, most prudish of men, was even more uncertain. Of course, when *The Midwich Cuckoos* appeared in 1957, everyone loved it. It sold and sold, and George Sanders appeared in the film version, to which a sequel was made. Nothing in either book or film could bring a blush to the cheek of a young parson.

As we rose to leave the café, Wyndham said, casually, "Well, I may write a novel about spiders instead."

Spiders were Wyndham's twitch.

Our paths crossed once or twice after that. Being a generous man, he had nothing of an older writer's hatred of the younger, and gave my story collection, *The Canopy of Time*, a warm review in *The Listener*. In 1965, we sat down and had a long conversation. We drank tea. After a while, when he had been vaguely complimentary and vaguely amusing, he invited me down to his cottage somewhere in Hampshire, saying, "Would you like to collaborate on a novel with me?"

One does not often get such magnificent offers. Should you, reader, ever get such a magnificent offer, I have a word of advice for you: Don't.

"Er – what's it about?"

"Spiders," he said.

Success meant little to him. He wanted to write a novel about giant spiders. Wyndham died in 1969. During that year, I was sitting in a café overlooking Copacabana Beach in Rio de Janeiro, talking to Frederik Pohl. Fred was then editing *Galaxy*, one of the best science fiction magazines. The subject of Wyndham came up.

Pohl gave a guilty start.

"I've just remembered that somewhere among my papers I have an unpublished Wyndham novel," he said. "He offered it me for *Galaxy*. It was too awful to run, even doctored. But I could not face telling John so. Somehow it got itself lost. I can't even remember what it was about."

"Spiders," I said.

Years after that – in 1975 – Michael Joseph published a posthumous novel by Wyndham, entitled *Web*. I need not say what it was about. It faded immediately from view.

Every writer has a twitch. A twitch is not the same as the *Lalla Rookh* syndrome. Sinking into obscurity and extinction is a natural process which we learn not to fear. Tom Moore enjoyed life no less because his book was read for only one generation and not five or six after his death. Twitches, on the other hand, can guarantee a writer's death while he is still alive.

I had a twitch. Such things are always irrational. For some reason, I wanted to imitate P. G. Wodehouse's silly-ass heroes. Bertie Wooster and the Drones seemed to me price-lessly funny. I looked for some way of introducing them into science fiction.

One result of this was two light novels which are neither one thing nor another, *The Male Response* and *The Primal Urge*.

But first there was *Non-Stop*. It was my second book, prov-erbially the difficult one.

This idea of the second novel being difficult originates from publishing experience.

In the fifties, every student in Oxford was writing a novel. It was about a young man from a privileged/underprivileged background who goes up to university, where he meets this wonderful female student with whom he has a wonder-ful/disastrous first love affair. So he writes a novel . . .

Later, in the seventies, publishers' offices were full of typescripts about a middle-aged women who finds her family has grown up and her husband is indifferent to her; she realises she has never expressed her real self or known real love. So she sits down to write a novel. At that moment, there is a knock at the door . . .

Times change contents, but first novels remain on the whole autobiographical. It is then difficult to know what to do for an encore. Real writers hurdle the gap; autobiographers often fall by the wayside.

Non-Stop and its successors have been autobiographical only in a spiritual sense. The lens for any kind of re-creation of reality is inevitably one's own life.

From what I have said of the story of *Non-Stop*, one thing is apparent. Everything that happens occurs amid hydroponic jungles rampant within a gigantic spaceship. It all takes place indoors.

I had found a way of balancing the two sides of my life, and of the conscious and unconscious. The jungle represented my secret longing for the freedoms of the Far East. The encasing spaceship represented the actual life I was then forced to lead. The whole also represents my interest in the processes of science – precisely the interest that cuts science fiction off from the ordinary novel, which only rarely embraces the concept of science as an integral part of our culture.

Looking back at the discarded Aldiss who sat writing in an upper bedroom of a house in Oxford, I am amazed by that image of the jungle bursting out and overwhelming everyday life. The ruined spaceship is haunting with its Piranesi vision of an enchained future. (Not of *the* future but of *a* future: the difference between definite and indefinite article here defines how integrally science fiction is a matter of language rather than hardware.)

One day, given the time, I might rewrite *Non-Stop*, to clear away a few unnecessary details, leaving the gaunt and uncompromising superstructure more clearly visible than I was able to do thirty years ago.

Just as the jungles of Burma and Sumatra came back to haunt me years later, so this novel still returns, for all its juvenile blemishes. I tried to put it behind me. Back it comes, some of its themes still reverberating through my fiction, though I never regarded consistency as my strong point.

When Faber & Faber published *Non-Stop* on 28 April 1958, I had cut the umbilical cord. I had said farewell to bookselling and become that immortal thing, that pariah, an independent author.

We are taught to regard our lives as a continuity. Yet I can look back on several discarded versions of myself, their life-cycles dictated from within as well as by external circumstance. The body continues, ageing, shaped by the sedentary life of a writer; perhaps the personality is discontinuous. Perhaps personalities live and die and others are reborn, all within the same ageing body, like Roy Complain and company within the giant ruinous spaceship of *Non-Stop*.

Following in SPB's Footsteps

The publication of one's first book is regarded generally as a miraculous event. Mothers, uncles, one's friends, the postman, the old schoolmaster, the man at the garage, all stand aghast at the prodigy in their midst. The author himself concurs with their opinion.

The second book naturally receives a less rapturous reception than the first. This is particularly the case if the second book takes place on what turns out to be a gigantic ship heading through space. The first sputnik had been launched in 1957. To most minds, the notion of *people* actually travelling in space was an impossibility not to be contemplated. For me it was an article of faith, and had been since childhood.

So the man in the garage fills one's petrol tank as usual. Bert the postman says, "Another book, eh?", and moves on to No. 71. One's friends smile and say, "When are you going to write another *Brightfount*, then?"

The response to one's declaration of independence, when one announces that the job is being thrown up and one is henceforth to live as a writer, with no other means, is more alarming.

Fathers are perennially concerned for the liquidity of their sons. My father's comment was, "If you can't stand that indoor life any more, why don't you become a postman?

There's a good pension at the end of it."

Even more worrying is when one's publisher advises one not to give up the job. Charles Monteith was always a mountain of tact. Even he rumbled a little when he heard my news. My agent was still more fervent. "Don't do it. It's ruination. You'll be broke in a year, like poor old . . . "

For a long while, I held in mockery my father's suggestion that I should become a postman. Writing was what I had always wanted to do, and he could have remembered that. Why deliver other people's communications?

But Father's life was not attended by the fortune mine has enjoyed. He was always frugal in his habits, a frugality I respect and recognise in my own sons. But, through misfortune, the frugality became miserliness. He drew in upon himself.

The war came. It was a time of shortages. My sister and I grew up in a period when everything was giving out. Favourite magazines disappeared because of the paper shortage. The saving of string was elevated to a national obsession. Sausages had to stretch. Nothing old could be thrown away. You served your country by not repainting your house.

All this played into Father's hands. How carefully he ironed and put away for next year the decorative paper in which the Christmas presents (oh, marvellous – *socks!*) were wrapped. If he stored away enough daily newspapers, to moulder in our air-raid shelter, Hitler would surely be defeated. A light bulb less, darkness at the top of the stairs, and we'd be home and dry. Parsimony became patriotism. The Dunkirk spirit was measured in five inches of bathwater.

After victory, how difficult the struggle through the late forties and early fifties, into a more competitive world. My father died in the mid-fifties, but lived long enough to hold my first book, my first son.

The day had a certain quality, the light an extra lucidity, when I no longer had to catch that 8.40 a.m. bus. To celebrate, I took the morning off, conscious that even that morning represented four hours away from the typewriter. The tyro writer is always aware that, while the typewriter is not clicking, money is drying like water in the desert, lifeblood is dropping into Earth's mantle.

In St Michael's Street stood a bookshop called John's, owned by the brothers Clutterbuck. John ran the paperback department downstairs, Brian the hardcovers upstairs. They did not get on well; their characters were very different. John was gentle and dreamy, and later took to mending violins and the laying on of hands. Brian was alert, humorous and high-tempered, and later took to supplying school books.

I went to see Brian. We had become friendly because both of us waged war against book thieves. Brian wore gym shoes (the forerunner of the modern trainer), in order to be more fleet of foot in pursuing thieves along the Cornmarket or down Ship Street.

When I told Brian I had left Parker's, he said, in his casual way, "I'll give you a job any time you want."

It was a friendly gesture. I regarded it as insurance.

These lines are being typed outside in the garden, on a table I had with me in Jugoslavia over twenty years ago. The sun shines. It is the first of October. Down in the vegetable garden, the remains of a bonfire smoulder, tanging the air with that sardonic Stone Age scent of smoke. One of our cats, old Foxy, sits by me. I am the grey-haired man who inherited the freedom his younger self earned, those many years ago.

The Times announces this morning the six short-listed novels for this year's Booker Prize. Four of the authors are known to me personally, Iris Murdoch, Jan Morris, Doris Lessing and J. L. Carr. When I last met Carr, only a fortnight ago, he was still holding against me, if jovially, the fact that I had once recommended the wrong publisher to him. He had asked me if he should send a manuscript to Collins or to Barrie & Rockliff. I answered Barrie & Rockliff. Carr claimed this decision condemned him to twenty years in the wilderness.

75

Why this judgment on my part? It seemed reasonable at that time, when I knew of an incident in which Collins had behaved coolly to one of their lesser authors, and when I knew a bright young editor at Barrie's. But Carr's grisly reminder (I had forgotten the incident and of course he had not) is an object lesson in caution when it comes to giving advice.

I did not become a postman as my father advised. Carr became a writer and publisher, and is this morning on the Booker short list. My novel *Helliconia Winter* was submitted for consideration, but has remained among the also-rans. I am happy to see Lessing again on the list. When I was a Booker judge, I was instrumental in seeing that her splendid *The Sirian Experiments* reached the short list; I experienced then (as if I hadn't before) the incomprehension and aversion which greets the mere notion of science fiction, even in supposedly enlightened circles.

After my conversation with Brian Clutterbuck, I returned home and began to write.

Regular writing to a timetable was essential at first. Now it is not. Then I worked more or less the office hours to which I had become accustomed. It was no hardship. I was buoyed with excitement, and rapt with interest in what I was writing.

In the last months of that busy year, 1955, I wrote a novella which I submitted to Ted Carnell. He accepted it promptly – his acceptances and rejections were always prompt. What he said to me was, "Since I am short of material for *Science Fantasy*, I am going to publish your story, but frankly you are wasting a great idea on such a short length. If you would like to turn the story into a novel, I will advise you and will try to sell it for you in the United States."

The story, "Non-Stop", my longest to date, appeared in 1956, with a cover illustration by Gerald Quinn, a cover to my mind as unconvincing as his enigmatic cover of orange shapes had been convincing.

With Ted's encouragement, but without his advice, I wrote the novel version. Of course he sent it to Faber, as related. He also sold it to America.

Carnell became an agent despite himself. He was in a position to see the difficulties Britain's science fiction writers were in. At that time, I was the only one of his regular writers who achieved the dignity of hardcover editions. The rest had to rely on paperback sales. The lower in the pecking order an author is, the more open he is to exploitation. The deeper the water, the murkier the depths. Some of those authors might have been able to write better if that had ever been suggested to them (or so one of them rather feebly told me); others were forced to accept low rates to keep themselves alive. Very few of those low-paying markets were as scrupulous as Ted with his *Nova* magazines.

Ted saw how his authors might sell abroad, given a good salesman. He elected to be that salesman, and founded the E. J. Carnell Literary Agency (now run by Pamela Buckmaster).

He was not the best of literary agents. He was as astonished as his authors when he made a sale. I remember once receiving an exuberant postcard from Ted, since he never wasted money on phone calls, announcing that he had closed a three-book deal with a Spanish publisher, and sixty-one pounds would soon be on its way to me. The deal signed over rights in my three best books. Ted never argued with any offer, as far as I know. He followed the old Hollywood advice, Take the money and run.

So he set about selling *Non-Stop* in that great Mecca, that great Babylon, of the publishing world, New York. And created a disaster area under which I have lived till this year.

I had every reason to hope for an American sale.

Most of the lively arts I enjoyed as a child came from the United States. While doing my best to evade joining Baden-Powell's Scout Movement, as I had evaded Sunday School and Choir, and was later to evade the Glee Club, I was an avid consumer of swing, jazz, boogie-woogie, popular songs, Hollywood films, American science fiction and other magazines – what the Germans rather condescendingly call *triviallitteratur.*

In *The Unembarrassed Muse: The Popular Arts in America*, Russell B. Nye has the following to say about science fiction:

> Science fiction has never been as popular as the detective-mystery, the Western, or the love story, but its appeal over the years has been surprisingly consistent. It can be used as a covert protest against the inadequacies and inanities of things as they are; it offers the future as an indirect attack on the present.

This was exactly how I felt and feel about SF. It should protest and offer alternatives to the discontents of our time.

My *Non-Stop* was an "unembarrassed" response to, a dialogue with, the science fiction I knew well. In particular, it was offered as a corrective to Robert A. Heinlein's two novellas, "Universe" and "Commonsense", with their unfeeling characters, which were published in John Campbell's *Astounding* (and later gathered as *Orphans of the Sky*). It was natural that my novel should have American publication.

Came another of Carnell's cards. He had placed *Non-Stop* at last. He had found a hardcover publisher for it, Criterion Books, owned by one S. G. Phillips. A contract would follow.

The contract duly arrived. A one-sheet job, brutally simple. I signed as instructed. I knew only Faber's honest contracts, Ted knew no more than I.

It was a contract with no release clause. As long as Criterion kept their edition in print, so long would S. G. Phillips take fifty per cent from any subsidiary sale, such as paperback or film rights.

When eventually some copies of the Criterion edition filtered through, my disappointment was great. The text had been altered, simplified. The title had been changed to *Starship*, which gave away the first major surprise of the novel, the binding appeared to be a kind of sacking, and the whole presentation was aimed at a juvenile or semi-juvenile market.

As I write, the Criterion edition is officially *still in print*. For obvious reasons, I cannot comment on that.

The paperback rights were sold to Signet, then a private company owned by Victor Weybright. Their science fiction list was edited by Truman "Mac" Talley, a sensible man who took an interest in his overseas author, and presented my first half-dozen novels to the American public under his imprint, all with covers which were quite striking for their time. All Signet monies for *Non-Stop* went through S. G. Phillips, to be delayed there, and halved.

Signet was bought up by Times-Mirror, after which dealings with the company were much more difficult. They let *Non-Stop* – or *Starship*, for it still bore the Phillips rechristening – go to Avon Books, who also paid over the royalties to Phillips. From time to time, on threat of law suit, some of this money reached me. Film options? All to Phillips, half eventually to me. Twenty-seven years after signing that original agreement, I managed this year to buy the Phillips company off.

Happily, Phillips had no say over foreign rights. *Non-Stop* has so far appeared in France, Spain, Italy, Slovenia, Denmark, Holland, Germany, Hungary, Japan, Norway, Brazil, Poland, Israel, Sweden, Portugal and Czechoslovakia.

With an Englishman's true instinct for failure, I have no business sense. My wife is methodical and keeps records. But a certain tenderness towards that first symbolic novel led me to make notes on its vicissitudes which I never bothered with again. They may now be of historic interest.

Faber's hardcover edition did neither well nor ill. It subscribed 2,276 copies. By June of 1960 it had sold 3,306 copies. Later, Faber reprinted it in hardcover.

Meanwhile, there was the question of getting *Non-Stop* into paperback in the UK. It sounds like a paradox these days, but appearing in paperback then was more difficult than in hardcover. It was finally accepted by a Manchester firm, Digit, through a lively young editor called Gareth Powell. Digit's edition was published in October 1960. It sold briskly, and reprinted twice, thanks to the enterprise of Gareth Powell, who went on to bigger things. Digit always paid sooner or later. I was grateful to them.

Paperback payments were not high at that time. In a year, they went up almost eightfold, to the subsequent benefit of all writers of the fantastic. John Wyndham was in part responsible for that.

In 1960, Penguin Books were at the height of their prestige. The sensational trial of *Lady Chatterley's Lover* was over. During the six weeks running up to Christmas, the unexpurgated Penguin edition of Lawrence's novel sold two million copies. England's libido was rising towards that distinctive climate, The Sixties.

In that year, Sir Allen Lane, the moving light behind Penguin, took on a whizz-kid to head the editorial team. The whizz-kid's name was Tony Godwin. Everyone knew Godwin, and respected him even as they dodged the chips on his shoulder.

During the summer, Lane and Godwin invited me to their London offices to have a talk. Lane was quite a handsome man, with the chilliest pair of eyes I ever saw. Godwin was sparely built, curly-haired and informal. Later, he became my editor at Weidenfeld & Nicolson. We got on well, both having come from a bookselling background and struggled for existence in a world full of university graduates, a facet of life which nagged Tony more than it did me.

Lane had daily sales figures on his desk every morning, something publishers rarely did in the days before computer print-outs.

From these figures, he and Godwin had observed two novels on the fiction list which sold as well and continuously as any Agatha Christie title.

Lane asked me about them.

"Do you know two novels called *The Day of the Triffids* and *Death of Grass?*"

"Yes. By John Wyndham and John Christopher."

Godwin asked me, "Would you say they are science fiction?"

"Yes."

"Is there any more of it about?"

The upshot of this conversation was that I was appointed editor of a new science fiction list, and commissioned to make an anthology of short stories. The latter duly appeared in October 1961 as *Penguin Science Fiction*. Combined with its two successors, it later became the *Penguin Science Fiction Omnibus*. That volume is still in print today, the longest lived of all SF anthologies.

For the list, I was able to introduce several American SF authors to the UK, and also to purchase J. G. Ballard's novel, *The Drowned World*. The payments set a new standard for science fiction.

There was another virtue of that list. Godwin had brought in a lively Italian art director, Germano Fascetti. Fascetti and I decided that we should break from the old stereotyped covers showing rocketships and so on. A Max Ernst adorned Ray Bradbury's *The Day It Rained Forever*, Klcc, Frank Herbert's *The Dragon in the Sea*, Picasso, Roy Lewis's *The Evolution Man*, Dominguez, my *Penguin Science Fiction*, and so on.

While my ill-paid *Non-Stop* was appearing from the Manchester publisher, decked out with a stale old American picture-cover, the new thing was happening at Penguin. It was a token of the general watershed of taste which the sixties brought with them: "the revolt into style", as George Melly phrased it. We may not have advanced far in public acceptance, but nothing will ever be quite as bad as it was before.

In 1964 I resigned from the position at Penguin to go to Jugoslavia. By that time I had begun to prosper. Tony Godwin left Penguin after a furious row in 1967. Sir Allen Lane died in 1970. He had brought in an irreversible change in public taste.

When you think how my generation depended on Penguin for entertainment and enlightenment – I bought a copy of Eric Linklater's *Poet's Pub*, Penguin No. 3, in 1935, and still possess the copy – there is no comparable publishing concern nowadays. Incidentally, many of Penguin's best continuing sales have been in novels which are unconfessedly science fiction or fantasy, such as *Brave New World, 1984*, and C. S. Lewis's Narnia books. Their Pelican list had opened with Olaf Stapledon's *Last and First Men* in two volumes. I managed to bring the Stapledon back into print in Penguin in 1963, after a long absence.

The years of the early sixties were difficult. Because I was adventurous and impatient, I refused to write the same novel over and over. Nor did I want to follow the habit of popular fiction, of having books with strong characterless heroes who carry all before them. My characters always had problems. This was what I enjoyed about the writings of those American SF authors who were never held in highest esteem at that time, Theodore Sturgeon, the highly amusing Robert Sheckley, and Philip K. Dick. They defied the rules and often wrote of jerks and renegades as central characters.

My reputation grew more rapidly in the States than in Britain, where enthusiasm is always in short demand and the cold shoulder fashionable. This was due in part to the marketing ability of Mac Talley and Victor Weybright and those good Signet covers.

One early morning in 1962, my girlfriend found on her doorstep beside her morning bottle of milk an object wrapped in newspaper, to which was attached a label bearing my name. She brought it round to my place that evening. It proved to be a Hugo Award for my "Hothouse" stories.

How it ever landed on her doorstep we never precisely ascertained. The Hugo is the annual popular American award for the best story or novel of the year. At that time I had scarcely heard of Hugos. My understanding was that they had to be vigorously campaigned for; I had done nothing of the sort. Here were big-hearted American fans showing they loved me.

Later it was demonstrated that small minds sometimes go with big hearts. At the time, however, pride was undiluted. It seemed that I was accepted by the American readership, where I belonged.

In gratitude, I began to prepare something really startling, something to shake the world.

Well occupied though I was, I missed the company of the staff at Parker's. I did not miss the customers; many university dons were snobbish and touchy. One was always polite in return, respecting learning, however deeply their libraries might be indebted to the bookshop. One particularly awful fellow had tried to get me sacked because I dared to argue with him over some Ordnance Survey maps. I never regretted escaping that sort of arrogance. Being independent means that one's health improves, as other authors have observed.

As for the supply of books: a new source was at hand.

The editor of the *Oxford Mail* in the mid-fifties was W. Harford Thomas. He heard that I was writing science fiction stories and sent for me. The paper was then receiving science fiction books for review. Harford Thomas had secured the services of an *Oxford Times* subeditor, Anthony Price, to review crime novels; Price had suggested that I might review the SF.

In the summer of 1955, many of the reviewers on the paper were away on holiday. I was stuck in Oxford in my palatial one-room apartment. I persuaded the editor's secretary, temporarily in charge of the books, to let me review a book on Freud and religion. From then on, I was allowed, within limits, to review whatever I pleased. There were always too many books, and those left over went to Oxfam.

Coincidences happen rather as in Anthony Powell's novels. These are the workings of fate, or appear to be. The literary editor of the *Oxford Mail* was none other than S. P. B. Mais, a grand old trouper whose name had been made in the thirties with broadcasts and many books. He was still writing, mainly for a publishing firm called Alvin Redman, now extinct. During the war, SPB had taught at the school where I was a pupil. He had hated the cold and discomfort of the place. When he left he wrote a rude book about it – to the delight of us poor scholars. To be caught with the offending book was to be beaten, if not expelled.

SPB was cordial as a result of this connection, cordial and amusing, and invited me to dinner. The Maises lived on the Woodstock Road. The first time I visited them, I caught him in characteristic attitude.

Theirs was a bay-windowed house. As I turned in at the gate, I could see SPB through the window. He wore his usual deerstalker hat. He was standing by a ping-pong table on which manuscripts were piled. He seized up one pile and threw bunches of papers madly about over his head, until the air was full of flying sheets. I heard him shouting.

Approaching the front door with some caution, I rang the bell. SPB himself answered. He was in his usual slightly irritable good humour. He spent that evening regaling me with stories of his friends. They included Robertson-Glasgow, who was a great cricketer and had broken the traditional pavilion clock somewhere.

SPB's wife Gill was in evidence. So were two lovely daughters, Lalagie and Imogen. SPB's routine was rather eccentric. He rose after lunch and stayed up, often in his dressing-gown, until ten of the evening. He then went to bed and slept until midnight, when he rose and worked until he heard the milkman. The clink of milk bottles was a signal to go back to bed. Nobody was allowed to make a sound in the house while he was sleeping.

The remarkable nature of this arrangement had an instant appeal. I scrutinised the faces of his daughters – no painful task – for any hint of resentment of their father, but discovered none.

At ten, I was thrown out. It was SPB's bedtime.

Later, when the two birds had flown the nest, SPB and Gill moved to a smaller flat, also on the Woodstock Road. I dined with him there too. He was good company.

Harford Thomas was a tolerant editor. He tolerated SPB as later he put up with me. Something in Mais's temperament always led him into escapades. He paid his rent by writing a series of articles about Oxfordshire for Harford Thomas. Those articles caused some problems.

One series featured Those Quaint Old Oxfordshire Pubs. The idea was that SPB would spend a morning or evening in some pleasant remote pub in Sutton Courtenay or Marsh Baldon or Great Tew or even, so help us, Kidlington, reporting later on events, conversations, etc. This he was supposed to do anonymously.

SPB was the least anonymous of men. Under his bookmaker's tweeds he wore four pullovers. Round his neck he wore three immense scarves, later donated to Dr Who. His countenance was choleric, his voice calculated to attract attention, to amuse, to exacerbate. He always phoned the pub well beforehand to announce his coming. In consequence, he generally got a good free meal and some free drinks out of the landlord, and met all the local rascals. The result was a lively article – and accusations of favouritism from other publicans.

Another series was less successful. SPB volunteered to write some articles on Oxfordshire Walks. He had once known the area well. He was not, in his old age, going to tramp the whole place again for a mouldy five guineas. So he cooked up the articles with the aid of memory and one-inch Ordnance Survey maps. Protests flooded in. How has he managed to walk through the new council estate at Watlington without noticing it? How could he see A from B, as stated, when Didcot power station was in the way?

The time came when SPB decided to retire from the literary editorship. He nominated me as his successor in 1960.

Another Mais coincidence occurred later. I recently bumped into Nicholas Shakespeare in the Groucho Club.

Nick has inherited good looks from his mother – who is one of SPB's beautiful daughters. Another legacy is an old SPB occupation, literary editorship, in Nick's case on the *Daily Telegraph*.

. A social note. In relating this story of pleasant, bustling old SPB, I must have suffered a lapse of memory. He cannot have written about a pub in Kidlington. The Kidlington pub in those days was a miserable place called, and rightly, The Dog. Driving through that village last week, I observed that The Dog has undergone gentrification and is now The Squire Bassett. It boasts little awnings over its windows. Let's hope the clientele is more amusing than formerly.

My routine as literary editor was to go into the newspaper offices, which were then in New Inn Hall Street, on Monday and Friday mornings and Wednesday afternoons. A company of us used to meet in a nearby pub for lunch on Fridays. This undemanding timetable continued throughout the sixties except for the months I was away in Yugoslavia, when my deputy, Jon Hartridge, who also wrote SF novels, took over the book page for me.

Years later, my wife and I were looking for a house – as we often were. We were being shown round a semi on Woodstock Road which was rather gloomy downstairs but attractive upstairs, with a balcony, when we realised we were standing in SPB's old flat, where we had once enjoyed beer and sausages with him and Gill. By then the old boy had been dead for some years.

SPB had lived perilously the life of an independent writer. Towards the end of his life, Gill shared writing duties with him for a series of travel books which Alvin Redman published, of which I now have only *Round Africa Cruise Holiday*. His name finds no place in Margaret Drabble's revision to that indispensable *Oxford Companion to English Literature*. His books on Shakespeare and Switzerland and Ireland and all the rest are one with Moore's *Lalla Rookh*.

Now I follow in his footsteps . . .

At least I never went back to work in a shop. By the end of my first year of independence, I had sold little, and the money in my post office account had all gone. Pride prevented my returning to take up Brian Clutterbuck's offer.

Slowly the tide turned. Those two trivial novels, *The Primal Urge* and *The Male Response*, were accepted in the USA.

This was an optimistic time, when various nations in Africa were being given their independence. Many of us hoped those nations, which had represented themselves as oppressed, would now rise and flourish. Nigeria in particular had high hopes riding on it, and the Nigerians were known to be friendly and sophisticated people. *Male Response* was set in a fictitious African country, Goya, and was a comedy of independence. I was pleased to hear that it had been well received in Nigeria and banned in South Africa.

Male Response was also a way, once again, of smuggling in something of my Far East experience. I still had a sense of being an exile in my own country.

CHAPTER 9

I Dream Therefore I Become

The mysteries of that ravenous ocean, the inner life, have proved a lasting fascination. This is why the subject of dreams and changed states takes up as much attention as other planets.

My current reading includes one of the great dream-state directors of the cinema, Andrei Tarkovsky, whom I had the privilege of meeting on one occasion in Rimini, when he told an enthusiastic Catholic audience of ten thousand people that what mattered was the individual, who remained always alone.

In his reflections on the cinema, *Sculpting in Time*, Tarkovsky speaks against pleasing audiences. "If you try to please audiences, uncritically accepting their tastes, it can only mean that you have no respect for them: that you simply want to collect their money."

Well, for us lesser mortals that is not always the case, since we may not rise above the level of taste of the general public. But certainly strenuous attempts to please the audience – which is generally an imagined audience – can preclude commerce with that mysterious inner world which alone has true value for us.

Once, at an IAFA meeting, I tried to promote this view, and spoke of a fear of the Scheherazade Syndrome – getting your head cut off if you fail to entertain. I said that one had the right to bore one's audience now and again. A female fantasy writer, listening to this heresy, was most annoyed. The audience, she claimed, must always be pleased. That's part of the deal.

It depends on what one thinks the deal is. SF was once impoverished by its isolation. Now it stands in danger of being impoverished by its popularity.

My inner life has always been a somewhat stormy sea. Sometimes I have feared to be overwhelmed.

In Thomas de Quincey's *Confessions of an English Opium-Eater*, he speaks of the visions he had to endure under the influence of opium:

> At night, when I lay awake in bed, vast processions passed along in mournful pomp, friezes of never-ending stories that to my feelings were as sad and solemn as if they were stories drawn from times before Oedipus or Priam, before Tyre, before Memphis . . . This I do not dwell upon, because the state of gloom which attended these gorgeous spectacles, amounting at least to utter darkness, as of some suicidal despondency, cannot be approached by words.

In the passage which follows that, de Quincey talks of the distortion of his time sense as well as his sense of space. "I sometimes seemed to have lived for seventy or one hundred years in one night, nay, sometimes had feelings representative of a millennium passed in that time, or, however, of a duration far beyond the limits of any human experience."

Such overwhelming impressions are not necessarily induced by opium or other drugs. In my early childhood nights, I endured similar torments, centred about distortions in space or time.

Of course no words can approach the terror of these dreams.

In one dream, I lay helpless in bed, knowing that a Deity

stood at the other end of the corridor beyond my bedroom door. That Deity was after me, for a reason of its own. It had merely to run down the corridor and snatch me out of bed. The Deity was flaming and terrible, like a vision from Blake's or Fuseli's paintings. It could run infinitely fast. It started running with a machine-like motion.

The distance of the corridor was no distance. Yet it was also infinite, a terrifying corridor at least as dreary and forbidding as the Deity. Only infinite speed could conquer it – and that the Deity possessed.

So the Deity was *simultaneously* very distant and up against my very door. The way he ran! – that irresistible velocity! – nothing could stand against it. This contradictory visitant I was forced to await, powerless, prone in bed, over several years, intermittently, though he never troubled me once I left that room.

Such dreams were torments. They were also poetical – poetical in the harsh way William Blake's illustrations to the Book of Job are poetical. In the drawing where Satan is transformed into an Angel of Light, he burns, entwined with the serpent, over a prostrate Job: "With dreams upon my bed thou searest me and affrightest me with Visions."

Although they affrighted me, I thirsted for those dreams. They were a form of vital communication with something within me which had no other representation.

Dreams enrich poor lives, even when they terrify. There is no terror coming from within us that we cannot withstand.

What was that Deity which could be both infinitely distant and burningly close? In waking life, we disregard the Big Bang which awakened us, the collision between sperm and ovum. From that collision, new life ascends to the molecular level like a fish rising to the surface of a river. We gather various levels of consciousness about us. After who can tell what epochs of eternity and timelessness, we emerge into the world beyond the womb, and are almost immediately expected to go to school and vote in general elections.

Perhaps that Blake-like entity was nothing more than my own awareness rushing to be roused, and re-enacting the grandeur of that primal collision, a ghost memory of my conception.

It must be in the interest of the life-force to remain open to such promptings from within. Myth, religion, literature – even literatures of a mean kind – seek to present dramatisations or interpretations of such moments. With such assistance, or unaided, or with drugs, or perhaps through the promptings of psychotherapy, we should strive to open the gates of consciousness wide. This occupation has little to do with amusing an audience.

"If hope for the better there be," said Hardy, "it exacts a full view of the worst." The distressing expanses of human nature revealed by Sigmund Freud have to be attended to, and digested back into the system, as it were. Knowing makes us whole.

Not everyone agrees with that view. Many wise men hold an opposite opinion. In an essay entitled "Shelley, Dryden, and Mr Eliot", C. S. Lewis says, "If a man will not become a Christian, it is very undesirable that he should become aware of the reptilian inhabitants of his own mind. To know how bad we are, in the condition of mere nature, is an excellent recipe for becoming worse."

There are dangers in all things; but if we do not despair in the quest of knowing ourselves, we need not fall into C. S. Lewis's trap of "becoming worse". Or I hope not. For it was not possible to become the sort of writer I became without more self-knowledge. The typewriter is much like a looking-glass; once you sit down before it in earnest, what you find facing you is yourself.

So strong was this impression, this sense of my own inadequacy in daring to address my fellow-men, that I took time off – that time which was like money which was like blood dripping down into the centre of the Earth – to write an analytical autobiography, which I called "Twenty to Thirty".

I needed to have clear before me my own virtues and short-comings. The document was intended for no eyes but mine. It provided some catharsis, though I had a poor opinion of myself, which I resolved to reform.

At the age of six, I had another dream which, though still time-related, was more mature in content. The dream recurred, with minor but significant changes, throughout my life, though since I was rash enough to write about it in *The Shape of Further Things* it became shy of appearing. I believe its function to be fulfilled now, since I have it no more.

The recurrent dream was one of comfort. I was a small, lonely figure, walking down a winding country lane, the hedges of which were cut low, so that I could see the country stretching to either side. Fields met my gaze, no sign of habitation. It was towards evening in the dream, with the sun low towards the western horizon.

A long way ahead, I perceived a church built of knapped flint, in the traditional English Perpendicular style, with a square tower – unmistakably a Norfolk church. I moved towards it. The sun sank lower.

As I neared the church, two people came from behind it to stand in the lane. Although they presented themselves in silhouette, the sun being behind them, it was clear they were dressed in old-fashioned clothes. The man wore a top hat, the woman a crinoline.

When I drew close, approaching the strangers ever more hesitantly, they came forward and were kind. They led me behind the church, to the far side, bathed in sunset.

The church proved not to be the solid building it had appeared from the lane. It was a ruin, a shell. All that remained standing was the tower and one long wall.

The fallen stone had been put to use. A cottage had been built with it, sheltering inside the arms of the church, its back wall in common with the church. In this modest dwelling the two old people lived. The front of the dwelling was rosy with the last of the sun, the front door stood invitingly open.

The couple welcomed me in. Birds flew towards the west. I entered – to find a fire burning in a grate.

This dream was immediately important. The first time it appeared, I set to with my crayons and drew the scene. The drawing was considered wonderful, to be shown to all and sundry.

One day I came upon a representation of the dream. I had returned to Sanders' bookshop to buy something. There hung one of Piranesi's *Vedute*, showing St Helen's Mausoleum in Rome. The classical building is in ruins; within its embrace, a modest villa has been constructed from the old stones. Washing is hanging to dry in the oblique rays of the sun.

The final shot of Tarkovsky's film *Nostalgia* also echoes my dream.

The ruins in my dream probably hold religious significance, and connect with an early sense of loss. The humble structure indicates that something, however small, can be built from what is left.

This dream has greatly enriched my life. Resonances from it still arise although the dream has died, like a recurrent theme in an opera. As I revise this chapter for publication, I reflect on a recent visit my wife and I made to Luxor.

We stayed in a hotel on the east bank of the Nile, overlooking that great waterway. From our room, we could gaze across to the west bank and the hills sheltering the Valley of the Kings. The ancient Egyptians believed that the eastern bank, the bank of sunrise where they lived, was the side of life; the western bank, the bank of sunset where their pharaohs were buried, was the side of death. Gazing across there in the evening, seeing the far hills turn rosy, I thought of the church dream that visited me early in life. Perhaps the sunset in that vision had a connection with the death of my older sister. Unlike her, I made the journey before nightfall.

Perhaps elements from the church dream reassembled themselves to give strength to *Non-Stop* and the components of the ruined ship; though that possibility occurred to me long after the novel was published.

This is a great power writing can bestow, if one is not merely trying to please some vaguely designated audience: to order one's own confusion, to strengthen communication with oneself. Mary Shelley puts the matter clearly in her introduction to the 1831 edition of *Frankenstein*:

> Invention, it must be humbly admitted, does not consist in creating out of a void, but out of chaos; the materials must in the first place be afforded; it can give form to dark, shapeless substances, but cannot bring into being the substance itself.

In several respects, my dream has proved predictive. I wonder if it does not carry within it another prediction yet to unfold: that when I am old I shall throw off my atheism and return again to the Church . . .

Dreams led me to the writings of Carl Jung. But that is a subject for a separate book.

In his pamphlet *On Dreams*, Thomas Browne of Norwich says that

> a good part of our sleep is peered out with visions and fantastical objects, wherein we are confessedly deceived. The day supplieth us with truths; the nights with fictions and falsehoods.

It is well put. But the day, or so it seems to one who reads his *Independent*, is equally well supplied with falsehoods. Trust to the night. Those visions lead back to something truthful.

A line or two further, incidentally, Browne has a word for De Quincey, when he tells us that "the soberest heads have acted all the monstrosities of melancholy, and which unto open eyes are no better than folly and madness."

Simply giving up my job and writing for so many hours a day did not make me a writer. What made me a writer was a realisation of my inner resources. Nevertheless, it is doubtful if I would have come to that realisation if I had not been free to take my time, and to spend whole days in a trance of introspection, or whole weeks pursuing lines of thought in books.

In this period, when I was sometimes down and out, I was remaking my inner character, doing a Victor Frankenstein and creating a new being out of the disintegrating fragments of the old. The lesson of "Twenty to Thirty" was learned. I changed. This is why the motto on my latest novel reads, "I think therefore I am: I dream therefore I become".

Anything new attracted me. Anything which would transform the colourless Britain of the fifties into the sixties attracted me. Tony Godwin was bringing many European writers into the Penguin orbit; they helped to make Britain less provincial. All Europe was reviving from the trauma of the 1939-45 conflict. The corpse was up and walking. In France, the *nouveau roman* was the thing. I read Alain Robbe-Grillet and Michel Butor and Marguerite Duras as they were translated. Butor's *Passing Time*, with its two converging time-streams, was interesting; but Robbe-Grillet's *Jealousy* was more extreme.

Robbe-Grillet and Alain Resnais collaborated on that startling film, *L'Année Dernière à Marienbad*, enigmatic, seductive, tantalising . . . just as their comfortless hotel is depicted as luxurious, baroque, lugubrious . . .

More than any other film, this one impressed me as both timeless and depicting a modern moment, in a limbo where there is always polite hostility and events are always enigmatic, where dream and reality meet. As strikingly as any spaceship, this static hotel was an emblem of our imprisonment.

I saw, too, a connection with science which was beyond the film-makers' intention. In my reading, I had just discovered Heisenberg's Uncertainty Principle, intimately connected with the unknowability of things on the quantum level. Link the method with the message, and one would have the perfect science fiction, in which elements of new science or supposed science were not simply dramatised within what was virtually a framework taken wholesale from the nineteenth-century novel of character, but would themselves constitute the framework of the representation. The so-called anti-novel had merely to be adapted.

The excitement! I would at last, single-handed, bring SF into the twentieth century.

The British literary establishment does not exist when we examine it closely. We find merely a number of people, some of whom may regard themselves as opposed to the establishment, some of whom have ideas which conflict in one way or another with their neighbour's, though all have various nodes of agreement. This is an application on the macrocosmic scale of Heisenberg's Principle, intended to be descriptive only of the sub atomic world. One characteristic predominates, however, throughout the establishment, a philistinism concerning science.

Since I have served on the Arts Council Literature Panel, have been chairman of the Society of Authors' Management Committee, have taken my turn as a Booker Prize judge, and so forth, I have also been mistaken for a member of that elusive establishment. But I have a liking for science as a path to understanding. I responded to Heisenberg.

The following passage occurs in *The Representation of Nature in Contemporary Physics* by Walter Heisenberg:

> For the smallest building blocks of matter every process of observation causes a major disturbance; it turns out that we can no longer talk of the behaviour of the particle apart from the process of observation. In consequence, we are finally led to believe that the laws of nature which we formulate mathematically in quantum theory deal no longer with the particles themselves but with our knowledge of the elementary particles.

Observation alters what is observed. The rule applies to the smallest building blocks of the brain.

I sat down to construct a fiction in which everything was observation within observation, and no ultimate reference point existed. Eventually a reference point was given – it takes the form of Holman Hunt's painting, "The Hireling Shepherd"; but whenever this painting is described, the description is different, so that we remain uncertain whether it is the same picture. The Hunt painting eventually featured on Faber's jacket for the novel, but it differs from the original in the Walker Gallery in that the girl in the painting has just set down (or is about to take up?) a volume lying open by her side.

In my novel, three observers, G, S, and C, each scrutinise the activity centring round a house through different instruments of observation. No resolution is given of the mystery. This was my *Report on Probability A*:

As a literary realisation of probability theory, *Report on Probability A* is a working out of the probabilities inherent in its structure and made known to us by the various ideas and concepts presented in the story in terms of its form. In other words, Aldiss demonstrates in the novel that "reality" itself is but a reflection of a probabilistic way of looking at the universe and that the novel is a literary realisation of what is implicit in probability theory. That which appears to be the real world turns out, after all, only to be a probable world with no way of ascertaining the reliability of one model, or interpretation of that model, or of another.

Let me leave that comment where it lies for a moment.

I completed the novel in 1962. I sent it to Faber. They rejected it. Through Carnell, I sent it to Robbe-Grillet's publisher in France. He rejected it. I sent it to Grove Press in the USA, then regarded as progressive. They rejected it. Carnell was not surprised.

So I forgot about the novel and got on with something else. It had been an experience to write; I should not wish for more.

Michael Moorcock is one of the most adventurous writers alive, a hero to his fans, a genius disregarded. In the sixties he took over the editorship of Ted Carnell's old magazine, *New Worlds*. When he wrote and asked me for a contribution, I remembered *Probability A*. The manuscript survived, despite my sojourn in Jugoslavia. Moorcock printed it entire in his magazine.

Faber were encouraged by this. They then felt able to publish it themselves. Their edition came out in April 1968. It is dedicated to Mike Moorcock.

Ordinary readers enjoyed the novel. I remember with gratitude tributes from Jill Tweedie and Robert Nye. The average science fiction reader hated it. I had hoped to please those who had awarded me a Hugo. Those very people saw *Probability A* as a betrayal of their trust. I received threatening letters about it.

That the novel saw hardcover publication in the States was due to a brave and perceptive editor at Doubleday, that great machine, called Lawrence P. Ashmead. Larry's name remains fragrant. He was a true friend of authors. He published not only *Report on Probability A* and *Barefoot in the Head* but also *Billion Year Spree*, three books which earned me hatred from American readers, three books which only Larry would have had the nerve to publish (as shown by the fact that all of them went to different paperback publishers in New York, and were bought for derisory amounts by Lancer Books, Ace, and Schocken Books respectively).

While working on a book, one gives it all one's attention. Once it is out, loose on the big wide world, it must take its chance. *Non-Stop* might appear to be an exception, but in fact for several years I forgot all about it; it was kept on the boil only by the rancour induced by the S. G. Phillips contract. I forgot about *Probability A* too, except to remember it as the novel in which I came nearest to fulfilling my original intentions before I set pen to paper. I loved it because it was despised, as one loves an unfavoured child. But I never bothered to open its covers again.

Not that *Report on Probability A* was exactly a failure. Sphere Books bought paperback rights in the UK, publishing it smartly on 3 December 1969. A good firm, Sphere; despite changes of editor they have kept *Probability A* in print ever since. There have also been German, Spanish and Japanese editions, and a splendid Swedish edition from Delta. The French will not touch it.

Publishers are not philanthropists. Nor are they natural allies of authors, although they can be that. Sphere have kept *Probability A* in print only because the novel still finds readers.

And readers are to be honoured. Though the initial reception in England was cool, many readers have come to me since and said, "Brian, I just read *Probability A* for the third (or sixth) time. What is there about that book?" This is a great merit of that much-maligned creature, the reader of SF; he or she will accept obscurity. He likes – or at least he *liked* – a challenge, and one trusts that the new wave of fantasy will not eradicate that trait.

But to my carelessness. My memory is no filing cabinet, like the awesome memories of some of my friends. Mine is a compost heap. Things get thrown there haphazardly, odd things sprout in the darkness. Over the years, I have been asked to speak about *Probability A*, and have trotted out something or other about "my anti-novel". Despite the title to remind me, I came to forget the Heisenberg connection. I had ceased to be deeply interested. It was past.

That last quotation, regarding the novel as a literary realisation of probability theory, comes from a volume by Frank Sadler entitled *The Unified Ring: Narrative Art and the Science-Fiction Novel*, published by UMI Research Press in Michigan. A copy has only recently arrived in my hands. Sadler discusses *Probability A* at some length – and I am embarrassed to be reminded that once I intended a completely new kind of science fiction, digesting its subject into appropriate form.

Unfortunately, just as the establishment is philistine about science, the bulk of the science fiction readership is philistine about literature.

That readership is also resistant to talk of art. The chilly reception for my innovative *Probability A* proved that I would have to work against the grain if necessary. My use of the Holman Hunt painting awakened an interest in deploying art, or works of art, within a science fiction framework, where they could operate as reference points to expand my hermetic universes.

Over several novels, to greater or lesser degree, I experimented with art metaphors. Not only in short stories but in such novels as *Barefoot in the Head, Cryptozoic*, where the chief character, Bush, is an artist, *Eighty-Minute Hour* where one of the male leads is haunted by a film in which he appeared some years earlier, and *The Malacia Tapestry*, which is an attempt to transpose the mysterious worlds of G. B. Tiepolo's "Scherzi" and "Capricci" into a kind of Renaissance romance.

It did not appear at the time that these novels added to my popularity; but I was too involved with the fascination of working out my themes to look further than the achievement of publication.

Of course one hopes that one's novels will sell when written. Only sales keep publishers interested. The act of communication is incomplete without the finished book, however much writing may be a kind of private communing. With short stories, risks are easier to take, since it does not matter greatly if a story occasionally fails to find acceptance. According to an esoteric publication, *The Illustrated Book of SF Lists*, I am one of the ten most prolific writers of short stories. Since *New Worlds* went out of existence, I have sometimes found difficulty in placing them.

Early in my career, when a collection of stories entitled *The Canopy of Time* was published by Faber, it received a laudatory review from a Cambridge paper. The review concluded by saying that my stories had "an almost classical perfection". Whatever the reviewer intended, I took this phrase to mean that the form of the stories was unadventurous.

The stories I then wrote took on different shapes, and became less to the received taste.

Among several veins of short story I mined from time to time, the enigmas pleased me the most. They developed from stories where technological advance was used as an aesthetic object and the point of the story concerned the difficulty of human relationships. A greater obliquity would be helpful, I felt.

Raymond Roussel, the novelist and dramatist who died in Palermo, used to make stories by joining up a list of random words. The landscape painter, Alexander Cozens – who may or may not have been an illegitimate son of Peter the Great – developed a similar method for creating landscapes, the "blot-tesque", in which accidental blots on the paper are used as stimuli towards the creation of a landscape. His book, published in 1786, refers to Leonardo da Vinci as claiming that the mind can be stimulated by looking at the stains on a wall and seeing pictures there. At the end of the last century, G. F. Watts, the almost forgotten English painter, conjured up his impressive "The Sower of the Systems" from similar reflections. And some of Victor Hugo's most interesting drawings and sketches are based on random wine marks or cigar burns on paper.

My method, if method is the word, was to break from a long piece of writing and scribble out on a separate sheet of paper half a dozen random words or phrases. These were set aside. Next morning, first thing, I would sit down and write a story round those words and phrases. Inspiration often springs from the arbitrary. The resultant stories I took to calling enigmas, a rather heavy-handed way of drawing attention to a vein of surrealism.

An enigma consists of three panels. Each panel is a picture rather than a story in the ordinary sense – a picture or perhaps an untoward event. The "story" lies in the unwritten relationship between the three parts; it may be profound or simply teasing. An area is left where the reader can invent for himself, an area of mystery unbridged by words. A recent example is "Her Toes Were Beautiful on the Hilltops", appearing in Robert Silverberg's "Universe" series.

The most successful of the enigmas is possibly "The Aperture Moment". Its three "panels" are "Waiting for the Universe to Begin", "But Without Orifices", and "Aimez-Vous Holman Hunt?" Some of these enigmas are gathered in the story collection, *Last Orders*. One day, they will all be garnered into one baffling volume.

C H A P T E R 10

Helping Writers — and Otherwise

An interruption. A break from the desk. A day in London. The Literature Board of the Council of Australia held a one-day symposium on Sponsorship in the Arts. This at the Commonwealth Institute.

It was worth attending just to hear how things are in other countries. The Australian position was outlined by Tom Shapcott, the Director of the Literary Board. David Peacock gave a résumé of the Canadian position; he represents Cultural Affairs in Canada.

Both Australia and Canada are much more vigorous in supporting writers than is the case in Britain – and matters have become worse since this symposium in 1985. Australia, through its Arts Council, is prepared to sponsor writers directly, or through publishers, or even booksellers. We listened with some astonishment to the story of a writer who had a sizeable grant given him in order to help him finish a novel. Further grants were given to his publisher, first to cover costs of printing the finished novel and then, later, to promote it. This is quite outside British and American experience.

The Canadian Arts Council has an efficient three-tier system from which all Canadian writers benefit.

In 1985, the British Arts Council sponsorship of literature almost ceased. Even the old Writers' Tours, which were good experience both for the writers and their audiences, are at an end. That is a great pity. Whatever the merits of simply handing out cash to individuals, the Writers' Tours provided stimulus and a chance for audiences outside London to meet the authors involved.

Both Australia and Canada fight to establish a secure sense of national identity. Their body of referential imagery is often externally derived, mainly from Britain and the USA. Authors like Peter Carey and Margaret Atwood are thus of much greater importance to their countries than they would be here. In time of peace, the road to identity lies in part through the arts, and in consequence the arts are well regarded. Recent successes in Australian cinema have been good for her image round the world; perhaps even Grundy TV's soap, *Neighbours*, has done no harm.

Arts have always needed patrons. They still need funding. Large sums of money are channelled into drama, opera and music every year, very little into literature. Which is curious, considering how much our greatest writer, William Shakespeare, earns for the country. In the complex modern world, old standards of supply-and-demand are too crass, though they still largely prevail in such outcast modes as science fiction.

A deal of well-informed rancour was aimed at the accountants who control funds for literature and believe that writers should be made as accountable as producers of a standard product. This is nonsense of a dangerous kind, though I remember from my time on the Literature Panel of the Arts Council a spectacular lack of accountability there. For instance, our predecessors on the panel had bestowed a fourth grant of money on a certain writer. This was to assist him in his researches on a book about whales. I asked if the book had ever appeared. No one knew. Had they enquired of the publishers involved? No one knew. The money had been shovelled into a pocket of silence.

Those who have a responsibility for handing out money

must hand it out responsibly. Dispensing money involves keeping accounts.

Class prejudice was also in evidence, since those who sat on the Arts Council panel were mainly middle class, or had become middle class and forgotten their earlier struggles. A friend of mine whom I had met in Liverpool applied for a modest grant for his amateur magazine; he was turned down. There were similar cases. The grounds on which applicants were refused were never clearly stated. When the long-lived magazine *Ambit* was turned down after receiving grants for several years, I tried to get it reinstated and could not; for no well-defined reason. A common experience of serving on that Literature Panel was one of frustration.

A writer can use a grant to buy time for his work or to pay his rent. Of course, he may simply drink it away or use it (in one memorable case) to buy new curtains.

I am against grants to individuals, particularly to beginner writers. What moves a man to be an author? Is it the desire to become another Elizabeth Bowen or a Rabindranath Tagore? Or is it a desire for independence, freedom from the system? Can you become a writer without that freedom? Can you enjoy that freedom if every book requires a handout?

The Royal Literature Fund, of which I am a member, is another matter. It exists to support the old and indigent writer.

At the end of this day of argument in the warm environs of the Commonwealth Institute, I was asked to sum up. I quoted Samuel Johnson's stinging rebuke to Lord Chesterfield: "Is not a Patron, My Lord, one who looks with unconcern on a Man struggling for Life in the water and when he has reached ground encumbers him with help?"

There had been a slight sense of encumbrance in even the most spirited contributions we had heard. With attention focused on getting more money for authors, no one had mentioned the Audience, though it was clear that both the Australian and Canadian administrations tried hard to

105

disseminate the native books they sponsored, not allowing them simply to drop dead on publishers' shelves. More attention must be directed to the Audience, Johnson's common reader; there is good evidence that an aversion to reading and better literature is not universal.

Even in the nineteen-eighties, we have seen in England how the Booker and Whitbread prizes have aroused interest in the modern novel. Such prizes are always open to criticism, but the public loves a horse race. Also, the experience of Penguin, who celebrated their first fifty years, shows hearteningly how people are avid for good books when the formula is right; nothing is too difficult for them.

A writer should say to himself, not, How can I get more money?, but How can I reach more readers (without lowering standards)? And this question is one which involves not only the writer but that antiquated structure, the Book Trade, riddled as it is with class conflicts, publishers against booksellers, booksellers against authors, and so on.

After this symposium, a small reception was held. We drank champagne and talked. Mark Le Fanu, the General Secretary of the Society of Authors, was present; he had involved me in the proceedings as Chairman of his Cultural Exchanges Committee. Also Charles Osborne, often reviled *éminence grise* of the Literature Panel of the Arts Council. Also Rose Tremain, who had regaled us earlier with an account of a gruesome year spent as writer-in-residence at a redbrick university. The university attitude to literature is very philistine. At Oxford, you have to be at least as dead as Hardy before you qualify for attention, unless you are a poet.

Although the attendance at this one-day event was small and, disappointingly, various Australian writers forgot to turn up, the proceedings were intensely interesting.

Yet as I returned home, I wondered that I had been so involved. After all, I am an outsider, and would never apply for a grant, or expect to get one.

Further reflection shows, however, that the situation is more complex than that. On three occasions I have been involved with the Arts Council and its disbursements. On the first two occasions, very successfully.

The first involvement was back in the sixties, after I had returned from Jugoslavia. Michael Moorcock was then running *New Worlds*, building it into an exciting magazine with an interest in all the vital arts then springing up. The old time-servers were kicked out. The fiction *New Worlds* ran was sometimes unreadable, but no longer a pale reflection of some past American mode. It strove to excel and break from its cultural confines.

As a result, Moorcock was soon in financial trouble. This despite the personal funds he pumped into his brainchild. I shall be surprised if I see again such dedication and energy as Moorcock, together with supporters like Charles Platt, ladled into that magazine. We used to have long phone calls at that time, while Moorcock poured out his troubles. On one of the occasions when things were desperate, I said, "Why not apply to the Arts Council for a subsidy?"

At that time, 1966, the idea was revolutionary. The Arts Council had taken literature under its wing only a decade before. Moreover, Moorcock and I had been brought up in the hard field of SF, where the rule was that of a Glasgow slum: it was the poor who helped the poor. We did not look to outsiders.

Moorcock let me campaign. I wrote to all those people who had at some time or another expressed a flicker of interest in science fiction, such as Angus Wilson and Marghanita Laski. Also Kathleen Tillotson, author of an excellent study, *Novels of the Eighteen-Forties*, who had written that the art of narrative had taken refuge in SF novels. Also Edmund Crispin, and several others.

Armed with their letters of support, I tackled Lord Goodman at the Arts Council. I went expecting to be bounced off the premises. Instead, they bestowed a generous grant and their best wishes.

So *New Worlds* No. 173 appeared in a new format in July 1967. It carried a cover by M. C. Escher, stories by J. G. Ballard, John Sladek, Roger Zelazny and Pamela Zoline (her exceptional story, "The Heat Death of the Universe"), poems by George MacBeth, articles by Charles Platt and Dr Christopher Evans, reviews by Aldiss and Douglas Hill, and the opening chapters of Thomas Disch's *Camp Concentration*, a novel embodying much of the spirit of the sixties magazine, with its savagery, darkness and literacy.

The second occasion of involvement was in the seventies, when I was one of a four-man Writers on Tour team sponsored by the Arts Council and sent to the north-east, to Sunderland, Durham and Newcastle. My clearest memory is of having to confront the fifth form of a comprehensive school at nine o'clock in the morning, after a heavy night.

The form room smelt like a ferret's cage. Not a very cosy ferret, either. The boys did not wish to speak or hear. It was an Us or Them situation. None of them read books.

I broke away from the dais and walked to the back of the class, where reliably the biggest louts were. Didn't they know what SF was? They were missing something. Had they never seen a science fiction movie? How about *Dr Who*? Stirrings of Life. Utterance, precious utterance. Laughter. Soon, you couldn't stop them talking. Some of them had even read A. E. Van Vogt. It was terrible to leave them.

Among the other writers on that tour was Bob Shaw. We strolled one morning in the Sunderland streets, talking of writing. We found we had both been attracted to the idea of a planet with a very long year, and setting characters down in the autumn of that year who would know that all their lives had to be spent against a steadily deteriorating climate. Five or six years later, having thought it over a bit, I started to write *Helliconia*.

* * *

The third Arts Council occasion was in the early eighties. The only academic institution in this country – in awful contrast to the USA – to give shelter to any official SF activity is a polytechnic, the North East London Poly, situated in Barking. The SF Foundation has an SF library and some facilities for students. As someone familiar with the Arts Council, I was approached by the Poly to try to secure a grant for an SF writer-in-residence. No such grant had ever been requested before. After the usual applications and interviews, I got agreement from the Literature Panel, and the matter was passed. The grant was generous as well as unprecedented. The Poly was pleased.

The post had to be advertised. Applicants had to be interviewed. Charles Osborne said he would be one interviewer; the Poly would provide three more; would I make up the fifth?

I said no. I knew all those who were applying. Many of them were my friends – the leading applicant had dined at my house, and so on. But nobody else came forward to do the job, so I was prevailed upon.

The position went to a man who did not really expect the job but talked about what he thought he could do for the Foundation; other applicants spoke only of what the Foundation could do for them. He blushed with apology when told he had the job – in which, incidentally, he was a great success. His name is Colin Greenland. He has since written several well-received novels and some excellent criticism.

Having claimed incautiously that the North East London Polytechnic is the only institution in England to sponsor any official SF activity, I must retract that slightly. The North London Poly in the Prince of Wales Road runs a lively H. G. Wells Society. Through its secretary, Chris Rolfe, seminars and conferences are held which attract many scholars, including some from overseas, such as Dr Julius Kagarlitsky from Moscow and W. Warren Wagar and Leon Stover from the United States.

Wells remains the great science fiction writer, with his amazing industry, the equal of Dickens', his imagination, his sense of fun. I would be in disgrace if I did not mention the society founded in his memory, and would probably lose my position as Vice-President.

Life is a series of interruptions. It is a week since I wrote here. I had to press on with another book. And there were other diversions – as always.

Since I am about to go abroad for a few days, I start to take an interest in the pile of unanswered correspondence on my desk, to wonder if something vital might be concealed there. There is a letter from two American writers, Jack and Jeanne Dann, asking me to write a story about Vietnam for their forthcoming anthology. Not knowing how to set about it, I have done nothing. Still, it was civil of them to ask.

I am setting the letter to one side, determined to drop them a line of thanks and say no, when the phone rings. Jeanne Dann, calling from Binghampton, New York. Did I receive her letter? Yes, I had it in my left hand . . .

Such a coincidence must mean something. Heaven knows what. I say I would love to write a story about Vietnam. Since I would be hard put to it to go into details of weaponry, etc., could I write a . . . well, say a fable?

That would be great, she says.

I say, I'll try, but stand by to be disappointed.

Directly I set the receiver down, the perfect idea arrives. The story begins with a troop carrier flying from the USA across the ocean to one of those R & R bases, a little American enclave in the midst of an alien land. The chief character, flown over in the troop carrier, is a native, not an American. The story is seen through his eyes. Although the US is for the South against the North, its vast wealth corrupts the South. The battle for hearts and minds is being lost.

The reader is some way into the story before he realises that the country invaded is not Vietnam but Britain.

How both countries get into this situation is part of the story. Progress is slow but steady. The narrative strategy is hard to work out, but extremely fascinating. It feels like a fresh thing to do.

Sunday evening of a beautiful October day. I read the new Doris Lessing novel, *The Good Terrorist*, with great interest, enjoying the portrait of Alice, the bourgeoise who hates the bourgeoisie. But a feeling of *being upset* eventually makes me drop the book.

Why am I upset? Tim has had his friends here all day. Five of them, all seventeen or eighteen years old, slept on the floor of his room last night. Others came during the day, bringing guitars, synthesisers, amps, and so forth. They are not allowed to make a noise at home; but we said they could play in our garage, since there is plenty of space all round us. Trees, still bearing their leaves, will absorb sound and protect the neighbours from amateur pop. We all enjoyed the day. After dark, a mother calls to collect one youthful musician. I chat to her. All parents think the Aldisses mad or heroic, since we always have their children here, putting up with their racket till all hours, feeding them casually on bread, biscuits, crisps, milk, the occasional bottle of wine. Someone's got to see them through the recessive eighties.

The mother says something about how do we survive?

I say something about still being able to write a few words (having worked on the Vietnam story between bouts of gardening).

Tim says, But music is more fun than words. And laughs.

Well, I think later, the thought getting between Lessing and my understanding, of course he finds his father a terrible bore. Ancient. One foot in the grave. All kids of eighteen do, one is given to understand. I don't care about that. Much.

I do care that he will never know the intense sybilline relationship with words, how words are a kind of counter-reality, a slide-show on top of the other slide-show, how words live in the head all day, like little serpents, pretty, dangerous, elusive. How I only really write novels for the sake of turning experience into words, the writer's Midas touch. Words play the magician. They transform me, they have transformed me. Much can be said against words. But this can be said for them. They are as inexhaustible as the oxygen in the air around us. And as essential.

Fun?

Yes, they're fun, too.

I have caught hold of them and turned them into my life's work. In turn they have enslaved me.

C H A P T E R 11

An Evening in London,
a Weekend in Nottingham

This chapter demonstrates the sort of things that go on in a writer's life when he is not actually sitting at his desk. It is also an occasion for name-dropping. But after all, we know a wide range of people when we have knocked about for a few years.

Yesterday was the day of the annual *Times Literary Supplement* party, the great all-chatting, all-drinking party of the literate, before Christmas. I was invited on the strength of having written one review (of Leslie Fiedler's book on Olaf Stapledon).

The party was particularly amiable this year, perhaps because Margaret and I had enjoyed a long lunch beforehand with Joan and Harry Harrison in their London apartment.

When I arrived at St John's Gate, the party was in full swing, the oak-panelled room already crowded. What a hubbub! I immediately saw some friends, including Alethea Hayter, with whom I served on the Committee of Management at the Society of Authors. She is wise, kind and acute in her judgment, and she wrote that inexhaustible book, *Opium and the Romantic Imagination* (and a few more, of course). I also talked to Victoria Glendinning, Eric Korn – whom I have known since his Oxford days and "The Cobra"– that notorious Indian restaurant – Redmond O'Hanlon, Andrew Motion, the jovial Julian Symons, Antonia Byatt, whom I much admire, and Beryl Bainbridge and Maggie Gee, who were sitting together in a corner. Beryl swore she would never leave Duckworth; Maggie and I were less vehement about our respective publishers. (I was in fact about to leave Cape.) Maggie Gee and I were judges earlier in the year in the *Daily Telegraph*'s Colour Magazine Mini-Saga Competition. I am the inventor of the Mini-Saga. A Mini-Saga is a literary form of precisely fifty words, excluding title. We received thirty-six thousand entries, because everyone thinks it easy to write a story in fifty words. We have run three competitions so far.

Here is an example of a Mini-Saga:

Happiness and Suffering

The doors of the amber palace closed behind the young king. For twenty years he closeted himself with his courtesan.

Outside, the land fell into decay. Warlords terrorised the population. Famine, revolution and pestilence struck, of which chronicles tell.

The king emerged at last. He had no history to relate.

The *Telegraph* has just had a film company make six Mini-Sagas into short films. I was neither consulted nor credited.

Judging with Maggie Gee and me was the ebullient Brian Redhead, one of the stalwarts of BBC Radio Four's morning programme, *Today*. Maggie reminded me last night that I had delivered what she claimed was the perfect put-down. Brian had been holding forth about his programme at some length. Apparently I then said, "Another boring programme is . . . ", and went on to talk of something else. I had no memory of this.

Sorry, Brian. Perhaps it was the drink.

Perhaps it was. Because last night I said something to Maggie Gee – and it was not a put-down – which made her drop her wine glass. It shattered to pieces on the floor and everyone looked round. To cover her embarrassment, I dropped mine as well. I had not meant to shock her.

Writers' paths through life are fraught with disappointments, some triumphs, and many set-backs, not to mention put-downs. Their work is often overlooked. So much brilliant work is now being done.

One of my hobbies is compiling a list of forgotten novelists. It is not easy to remember forgotten novelists. Eric Linklater, once a great favourite, Patrick Hamilton, A. J. Cronin, Ian Hay, Eden Phillpotts, Gabriel Fielding, David Stacton, Alejo Carpentier, author of the masterly "The Lost Steps". And many more, enduring the fate of the author of *Lallah Rookh*.

In Wallingford the other week, I bought a few volumes of Leonard Merrick, whose writing pleased several lifetimes ago. I am reading *Conrad in Search of His Youth* with a deal of "quiet enjoyment", which is to say, not much enjoyment at all, though I have adopted one of his epigrams for a novella now in progress. No writer these days could get away with Merrick's dilettante performances.

But how did I jump from the October of last chapter to the December of this? Work and necessity intervened.

Much has happened since that day when Jeanne Dann rang from New York State and prodded me for a Vietnam story. The Danns were pleased with the results. I called it, "My Country 'Tis Not Only of Thee". Judy Cooke – also at the TLS party last night – accepted the story for her *Fiction Magazine Anthology*, where it is rechristened "Vietnam Encore".

Since October, there have been two more trips abroad, one with Margaret. We flew to Toronto, to the Harborfront International Literary Festival, where I did a reading. More recently, I was over in Madrid to do a five-hour marathon TV (La Clave) show on the future of Automation and Artificial Intelligence.

In the Prado, I saw visitors picking at a Bosch painting to

establish whether it was painted on wood or canvas.

Later, and another literary event. The Society of Authors organised a writers' symposium in Nottingham. It was a weekend affair at which a few of us were invited to address an audience of about a hundred and fifty – all of whom were, or aspired to be, writers. All such aspirants should join the Society.

We all stayed in the university, except for Maxim Jakubowsky, who sensibly installed himself in the Moat Hotel in town. It soon became clear what a gulf lay between the real writers and the aspirants. While the help that can be given on such occasions is limited, conferences are often an end unto themselves, their posited goals little more than pretexts for a get-together.

We met on the Friday evening over red wine. The first session was a forum, "Keeping Up the Work Rate". As opening speaker, I mocked the title, with its suggestion that authors were a sort of production line who had to turn out so many words a day.

It was easy enough to become a writer: the real problem was to continue one, to continue to derive pleasure and revelation out of a lifetime of writing, since once authorship is entered into there is often no escape from it. Later, I realised the unintentional cruelty of this observation; getting to know the audience better, we realised the extreme difficulties some people experience in becoming writers. Was it a question of talent or luck?

I asked the audience to consider if it was not likely that some psychological types were better suited to the peculiarities of an author's life than others. I referred to the book already mentioned, Anthony Storr's *The Dynamics of Creation*.

Dr Storr talks of manic-depressives who have become successful and productive authors. The very irregularity of an author's life suits their temperaments. They can work in bursts of energy and be content.

One of Dr Storr's examples is Honoré de Balzac.

Balzac was a great producer who decided early in life to be a writer. Frenzied bouts of writing were interspersed with orgiastic periods when Balzac ate and drank wildly. His relationships with women were as frenzied as his relationships with his manuscripts, which he attacked and altered even when they had reached galley and second galley state. No printer today would tolerate Balzac's madness.

His biographer, Stefan Zweig, says, "With the exception of Beethoven's notebooks there are hardly any documents existing today in which the artist's struggle for expression is more tangibly demonstrated than in these volumes." Zweig refers to massive volumes of proofs, sometimes consisting of two thousand pages, which Balzac had bound to present to his friends as the most precious gift he could bestow.

Zweig relates how much of Balzac's life was poured out on paper. He could enjoy freedom for only a few brief hours, then back to his desk, his sacrificial stone. His contemporaries understood little of his real nature.

Everyone should read Zweig's book. Every writer will tremble. The last word is Dr Storr's. After explaining that Balzac killed himself by his manic activity, he adds, "The remarkable thing about his activity is how effectively it did protect him."

If you have the temperament to be a writer, then you will be as happy as it is in your nature to be. If your temperament is unsuitable, you will be miserable. Do something else.

The natural writer cannot imagine himself or herself living in any other way: for ultimately the question is one of being rather than doing. This I tried to tell the Nottingham audience; but what most of them wished to hear was how many words they should write a day.

Jonathan Raban spoke next. He and I had met at the Toronto Harborfront Festival when, blissfully happy, he had sailed on Lake Ontario. Jonathan is urbane, cultivated, amusing – all the things we should all like to be. He made my error of misjudging the audience. He advised his listeners to treat each book as a partnership between author and publisher. Don't be mean where publishers are concerned. It is all very well to accept your editor's lunches, but you should take him out occasionally, as one would a friend. The audience sat quiet; what they wanted to know was how you got a free lunch off the blighter in the first place.

Not all our listeners were novices. Two of the women writers were tax exiles in Ireland, earning a great deal of money. The advice they wanted from us was how one achieved some critical consideration. Some writers there had had several books published and not a single review.

I had a conversation with a lady who wrote historical novels. She specialised in one particular century. Her first novel had been published in the seventies. It sounded interesting, and I asked her how many novels she had published since then.

"I've written six more, but I haven't been able to get them published as yet."

It would have been too glib to advise her to try another century.

One of the most amusing speakers at the symposium was Brian Ford, who delivered several peppy addresses, exhorting his listeners to be more forthcoming.

"Don't say to your editor, 'Let's meet outside the Pig and Whistle and we'll sink a jar.' Treat him the way you'd like to be treated yourself. Tell him to meet you in the cocktail bar of the Savoy, create a successful ambience for yourself. Go out to people who are, after all, your customers."

But what the audience wanted to know was how you got hold of an editor in the first place, and where the Savoy was.

On the whole, Jonathan, Brian and I only succeeded in making the struggling authors feel more depressed. So I thought, driving home.

Generally the would-bes were modest, even deferential, something one never expects from a science fiction audience. At the end of each session, during the question-and-answer period, the professionals stood up from the audience and contributed a statement, or perhaps contradicted something that had been said by the panel. The other members of the audience contented themselves with small questions.

"Does it matter what time of year your book is published?"

"Should you ring your publisher, and if so, is morning or afternoon best? Mine always sounds so terribly *busy*."

"How would you go about getting a book published abroad?"

By these small tokens, they registered their contribution to the proceedings: a freight of anxiety.

They were stout in defending English decencies. The last panel of all was entitled, "Getting the Best out of Your Publisher". On the panel for that session was a man who introduced himself as a member of the Writers' Guild. I had never heard of him, and cannot recall his name now. He began by saying that if he had had his way he would have called the panel, "How to Best Your Publisher".

Perhaps the remark was made in order to raise a laugh; true, it raised a titter, but it was very unpopular and the next speaker on the panel, William Horwood, was quick to dispute it. I cannot see any successful author behaving in the suggested manner. Besides, publishers are not easy to outsmart.

The author-publisher relationship is a difficult one. It can be very rewarding, but rewarding, in the main, I believe, for the author, who by the nature of his work is more isolated than a publisher.

Brian Ford's metaphor is a telling one. He says that the author-publisher relationship resembles an apple tree, the tree being the publisher and the apples, the fruit of the tree, the authors. When an apple falls, the shock is considerably greater for the apple itself than it ever can be for the tree.

I left on the Sunday evening feeling doleful. Perhaps everyone else did. Except the ever-cheerful Brian.

CHAPTER 12

White Hopes, Black Olives

In 1961, I went to live in a small terrace house in a street running between the Iffley and Cowley Roads. I bought it from a friend on the *Oxford Mail*, Anthony Harris. It had a room and a kitchen downstairs and a bathroom and two bedrooms upstairs.

At the rear of No. 24 was a small and private garden with a pool in which four goldfish drank deep of life. A tool shed stood on the lawn, covered in clematis montana. Behind the far wall was a secret, or at least secretive, passage, along which could be heard the slap-slap of sandals on flagstones.

Off to the right as one looked down the garden, as one often did in search of inspiration, was a church. Off to the left was a dormitory-house where a religious community, the Cowley Fathers, lived in conditions, so one hoped, of extreme sanctity. The secret passage connected house with church. And the sound of the fathers' feet as they went to worship was like the sandalled approach of fame.

At the far end of the garden I placed a galvanised iron washtub on its side, with a tin can standing in front of it. I used to shoot at the tin can from the kitchen door with an air pistol. This target practice was my exercise, together with the thrice-weekly walks up the High to the *Oxford Mail* and back.

I did a lot of work in that friendly little house, and got

myself out of debt.

At the same time, another new personality was being born, to flourish in the exuberant atmosphere of the sixties.

Days were monastic in No. 24, evenings gregarious. With C. S. Lewis, I was an initiating member of the Oxford University Speculative Fiction Group, the leading lights of which often visited me. One of them, Chris Miller, virtually lived in for a while.

During the day, I enjoyed my solitude, existing on a diet of coffee and Melton Mowbray pork pies. I played a lot of music – often Ravi Shankar, who was big then. Ravi Shankar went with the sandals. A decade earlier, when I had felt myself imprisoned, when I was a wage-slave, I had played Borodin, to remind myself I had Byronic depths, or at least Byronic shallows.

Deep into the night at No. 24, when I could not sleep, I listened on my Bush to Radio Free Europe, which originated from Frankfurt. One programme in particular I enjoyed because it began with echoing footsteps and an announcer saying, " . . . quiet listening, and the lonesome sounds of a city after midnight . . . " Being awake at three in the morning is the next best thing to getting stuck in the middle of the Gobi when one's faithful dromedary has broken down.

Airs of Earth was a collection of stories appearing in 1963, rather remote in its concerns when one considers that, in England, this was the year of the Profumo affair, the Stephen Ward Case as it was then known, a scandal that brought down the Macmillan government. All Britain – and not Britain alone – was agog for more news (and more pictures, please) of the two young ladies in the case, Christine Keeler and Mandy Rice-Davies.

A rigidity in English society was breaking down. Christine Keeler was a catalyst in that process. She was highly attractive sexually, a slender girl who seemed to promise instant availability. And she larked naked with the nobs at Cliveden, home of the Astors, venue of the smart set. Such ladies act as a magnet for many of the emotions pent up by society.

When we arrived in Jugoslavia, a year later, we saw in a scrubby little bookshop in Maribor a book on the Stephen Ward Case, published in Slovenian. The scandal had travelled far and fast. To a Communist country, of course, such decadent capitalist goings-on were meat and drink.

In 1964, two novels appeared. *The Dark Light Years* had a new assurance and zest marking a new phase in life. It was followed by *Greybeard*. *Greybeard* is set in Oxford and the country thereabouts. Some episodes take place in Swinford, by the anachronistic tollbridge which still remains; an artist friend, Oscar Mellor, lived there in those days. Other scenes are staged in Christ Church and Balliol, which are at war with each other. It's an elegiac novel, my attempt at a Thomas Hardy, full of the English countryside and a sense of the precariousness of human life, and is dedicated to my two older children, Clive and Wendy.

Earthworks appeared in 1965. A young fan and writer called Charles Platt criticised it savagely in *Tomorrowscope*, a magazine which had a circulation of less than a hundred copies. My copy, arriving in the post just before publication day, completely cooled me towards my novel. I must have been very thin-skinned. Charles has long been a valued friend, but I have never warmed to *Earthworks* since that occasion, not even to the latest Grafton reprint, with its attractive cover.

Well, possibly *Earthworks* is slightly depressing, though that can hardly have been Charles's objection, since his own novels stay pretty firmly in the mire.

From the United States came many complaints that my novels and stories were "too downbeat". *Frankenstein Unbound*, for instance, was rejected on that score. The Americans are learning irony nowadays, and the complaint is heard less often. However, SF, even American SF, has a tradition of scepticism and melancholy, best embodied in the writings of Philip K. Dick.

Happiness and unhappiness lie close; though opposites,

together they form the binary system of subjective life. Melancholy has its pleasures. Also, it is worth remembering what Samuel Johnson said on the subject: "To tell of disappointment and misery, to thicken the darkness of futurity, and perplex the labyrinth of uncertainty, has been always a delicious employment of the poets." Perhaps Johnson was thinking of his own *Rasselas* when he spoke; it remarkably "thickens the darkness of futurity".

Faber published a collection of short stories, *The Saliva Tree*, in 1966. The title story is by way of being a tribute to H. G. Wells, and was popular, although it is the other stories in that selection, like "Girl and Robot with Flowers", which mark decisive developments. But *The Saliva Tree* won a Nebula Award the first year those prizes were instituted. Margaret and I flew to New York to collect it.

The Saliva Tree is an example of a story which got written because its title dangled before my eyes, waiting to be used or abused. The trail began in Trieste.

The city of Trieste is sunk deep in a history from which it has scarcely managed to extricate itself. Its population is almost as mixed as that of New York or Cairo. It was once the port of the Austro-Hungarian Empire. In the south-western suburbs of Vienna, among the prevailing greys of that museum city, you may still come across Café Trieste, the Adriatische Restaurant and Triestestrasse. Between Austria and the city of Joyce and Svevo a wary Communist nation has been interposed; the Treaty of Versailles, at which Austria-Hungary was dismantled, saw to that.

During the interregnum between the two world wars, Trieste was a free port, and the scene of many riots. At the end of World War II, General Tito and his partisans attempted to seize the city. New Zealand troops moved swiftly in, to confront their erstwhile allies over the barricades. Eventually, Tito retreated to the scrubby *karst* hills that lie behind the city.

It was not until 1954 that the country south of Trieste, around Koper (once Capodistria), and Piran (Pirano) with its little statue of Tartini in the main square, was finally ceded to Jugoslavia, while Trieste was finally ceded to Italy. In 1963 an annual Science Fiction Film Festival was founded in Trieste.

It happened that I reviewed science fiction films for the *Oxford Mail* at that time, and had had an article published on the subject in an Italian magazine; so I received an invitation to that first festival, and took my girlfriend Margaret along. Ted Carnell also went, and Kingsley and Hilary Amis, and Harry and Joan Harrison, who were then living in Denmark, in pleasant Rungsted Kyst, once home to Karen Blixen.

The previous year, we had visited Joan and Harry in their Blixenesque hideout. We were poor as country mice; Harry was writing the script for Flash Gordon strips and working on his great overpopulation novel, *Make Room! Make Room!* . . . It was my first journey abroad since my years in the Far East. Trieste was the first trip back to the sun.

Trieste was amusing. With Harry and Kingsley there, it could hardly be otherwise. A lot of drink went down, from Asti Spumante, Campari and grappa to other unnamed local vintages.

Between the sunshine and the alcohol and the awful films, the three of us began to cook up a science fiction novel we planned to write with Bruce Montgomery. Kingsley's idea was that it should contain something subversive and shocking, like institutionalised cannibalism. Fit young men and women were being bred up for the table. We even had a title, "The Saliva Treatment", invented amid gales of laughter.

This round-robin novel never got written. But some years later, Margaret said, "What about that novel?"

"What novel?"

"The one you kept talking about in Trieste. 'The Saliva Tree'."

It struck me that we could not have been particularly lucid in our enunciation if all she had heard of the title was "The Saliva Tree".

So I set myself to write something with that name, to

commemorate a good holiday.

I served on the jury of the Trieste Film Festival again in 1970, with Guido Piovene as President, and in 1974, with Alessandro Blassetti as President. On the latter occasion, when we had a Soviet film producer, Ivan Boclorov, on the jury, proceedings were very stormy. Harry and Kingsley were much missed then. The festivals ceased in 1982.

In 1963 all was sunshine and monkeyshines. A Jugoslav, Josef Dolničar, affectionately known as Joe the Jug, showed us round Trieste and the shadier drinking spots. Joe was the first of a sturdy band of Jugoslav SF readers I was to meet over the years.

Harry, ever resourceful, had driven to Trieste from Denmark, via Schleswig-Holstein, with Joan and their two kiddies. At the end of the festival, he said, "How about a trip into darkest Jugland?" Oh dear, Harry, what you started . . .

We shopped first in Trieste market, down by the rather abbreviated Canale Grande, and drove south in Harry's trusty Volkswagen van, which had no petrol gauge.

The sun blazed down. We roared into the hills of Istra, which the Italians called Istria. I asked Harry what the history of the Istran peninsula had been.

"Too terrible to contemplate, Brian. Don't ask."

Typical Harrison reply. Possibly a cover-up, you might suppose; but, if so, Harry filled in the background later by talking to a Croatian coalminer in Esperanto and getting the dirt from him. The man said the history of the Istran peninsula was too terrible to contemplate.

Istra is beautiful. We've often been back. Inland, it is haunted, with ruinous towns perched on eminences, tenanted only by goats – perfect proof of Harry's dictum. I put one such town into my novel, *Life in the West,* many a year later.

We drove into the hills near Pazin. There, on a bend of the dusty road, we found a pleasant old stone *gostilna,* sheltered by vines, with hens clucking on the grass. We stopped, ordered the local wine and spitted chicken, and the women went to find the Ladies.

They came out screaming. "It's awful! It's awful!"

Harry and I rushed in to inspect, to smell. We had both survived the army, in Texas, in India.

"That's nothing," we said. "Luxury. Spotless."

Food was served on benches in the open, under vines. I trapped a cicada under an upturned glass for Harry's son, Toddy. Ah, what happiness! To be back in the sun! It had been sixteen years since I had enjoyed the southern heat. The simple food and drink were delicious. What epitomised that meal, that whole day, was the great pannier of black olives set on the table: large, sumptuous, fruits of sun, tasting as only olives can.

Jugoslavia! Jugland! What a magnificent country!

As soon as we were back in England, I set about acquiring some knowledge of the Balkans. I started to learn Serbo-Croat, and to negotiate with the sticky Jugoslav Embassy in London. During the years of the Cold War, it was not an easy country to enter for any length of time. However, I got a commission from Faber to write a book. I learned to drive – I had always been too poor to own a car. I bought a second-hand Land-Rover. On 4 March 1964, I set forth again with Margaret (a good driver), only eight months after the trip to Istra with Harry.

There is still mystery about Jugoslavia, despite all the thousands of tourists who every summer line the Dalmatian coast, to fry on its rocks. In 1964, it was almost a closed country, rigid under Communism, wary alike of East and West, belonging to neither. At the turn of the century, much of it had formed part of the Ottoman Empire; Sarajevo, when we reached that city, had seventy incontrovertible mosques. In the museum in Sarajevo a strange long metal instrument was displayed; it had been used to dose camels – and who knows, perhaps their drivers – when they arrived at the city *han*, sick from the long trail leading eastwards to Bukhara and the old silk route to Xian in China.

126

In *Eothen*, Alexander William Kinglake begins his story as he crosses from Hungary to Belgrade, at the place where the Sava River joins the Danube in its eastward roll. This, by the reckoning of the 1830s, was where the East began. His book opens with this wonderful paragraph:

> At Semlin I was still encompassed by the scenes and the sounds of familiar life; the din of a busy world still vexed and cheered me; the unveiled faces of women still shone in the light of day. Yet, whenever I chose to look southward, I saw the Ottoman's fortress – austere, and darkly impending high over the vale of the Danube – historic Belgrade. I had come, as it were, to the end of this wheel-going Europe, and now my eyes would see the splendour and havoc of the East.

The splendour and the havoc of the East . . . Well, my eyes too have seen those sights, and it is one of the things in my life for which I am most grateful.

As a result of our Jugoslav journeyings when, in the course of half a year, we covered all the republics of that nation from the Vojvodina in the north, with its flat plains and open skies, to the secrecies of Macedonia and Lake Ohrid in the south – Ohrid, with the dark mountain fortress of Albania standing out across the water – I produced my one travel book. We lived like gypsies on bread, salami, cheese, local wines, camomile tea and slivovitz. *Cities and Stones* was published, illustrated with our photographs, by Faber, on 24 November 1966.

Talking to Harry of that long excursion some years later, I said, "It's a funny thing, but in all our travels we never came across any luscious black olives such as we ate that day in Istra. The Jugs grow only green olives."

"Didn't you know?" he said. "I bought those black olives in Trieste market before we left. Only the Italians know how to grow olives . . ."

* * *

The sixties rolled happily on.

In 1967 Faber published a novel called *An Age*, which later became *Cryptozoic*. Parts of that novel are better than the whole. But it is very fantastic and contains fine arid landscapes. I imagined myself back into the far past. It was another self-contained world; they were to be less frequent from now on.

Science fiction was undergoing one of its periodic revolutions, and the first to be generated in England. Mike Moorcock at *New Worlds* was throwing out the old guard and setting the Thames on fire.

I had a passion for science fiction. I once loved it more than any other kind of writing. I read *Astounding* from 1939 until at least 1954 with avid intensity; indeed, in a life of reading many kinds of literature, devouring that monthly *Astounding*, as edited by John W. Campbell in his heyday, was my most intense reading experience. That was why I had a contempt for weary writing and second-hand story-telling in Carnell's *New Worlds* and its sister magazine, *Science Fantasy*. Moorcock threw that gang of cribbers out.

There had been one writer whose early stories I admired. He too was a Carnell protégé, if protégé is indeed the word. His name was J. G. Ballard. No one rivalled him, from his first story. I consider it fortunate that there were two writers in the field close to me like Ballard and Moorcock against which to measure myself.

Ballard, Moorcock and Platt formed the core of what became known as the New Wave. It coincided, give or take a year or two, with the rise to popularity of the Beatles, and marked another example of "the revolt into style". It accorded with the times, when Harold Wilson was Prime Minister and all was well, and was later taken up by writers in the States.

I was one of the first to draw attention to Ballard's unique writing, in a short-lived little magazine I co-edited. That came about in the sort of indirect way in which things happen.

In 1961, Moorcock and others started up an organisation

called the British Science Fiction Association. It is still going strong. The BSFA is the place to be if you are interested in science fiction and wish to play some kind of active role. I was elected its first President, and reviewed books for its magazine, *Vector*.

One day, I was sent for review the paperback edition of Robert A. Heinlein's *Starship Troopers*. The novel was already notorious. *Starship Troopers* is a violent tale of interstellar war – and how those troopers love their dear brutish sergeant. It was the work of a man who had never been to war. I hated its sentiments and its sentimentality. My review began, "This is the third-rate novel about which there has been all that fourth-rate discussion."

The review brought me brickbats, and a letter from Harry Harrison in Denmark giving me a cheer. He wanted more honest criticism of this sort. At his instigation, the two of us started the magazine of criticism, *SF Horizons*, with Tom Boardman Jr as our energetic business manager. Tom later became my business manager for a while. In the second issue of *SF Horizons*, I wrote an article praising Ballard, comparing him with other British writers, saying, "They are copying; Ballard is originating." He has remained among our most original writers.

So I became involved with *New Worlds*, though no part of the coterie that flourished in London – more particularly in Mike's home in Ladbroke Grove.

At the same time, I was travelling more. Freedom to travel is one of the benefits a writer earns for himself. As the New Wave washed across SF, so the idea of Flower Power and Swinging London washed over Europe, and then the States. I began contributing a series of "Acid Head War" stories to *New Worlds*. Often these stories were written as I travelled the ground, in Scandinavia, Belgium, Holland, Germany or England, written in an associative style laced with holophrastic paronomasia.

One of my readers said to me, "This isn't the future – it's

happening now."

It was. The New Wave discovered the miraculous present.

The Acid Head War stories, considerably revised, appeared from Faber in 1969, with a splendid cover I chose myself, as a novel entitled *Barefoot in the Head*. It was published by Doubleday in the States in 1970, thanks to Larry Ashmead. Charteris, the central character, is too busy with drugs, God and rhetoric to observe the quietly loving woman by his side. *C'est la vie* – and not only *la vie des soixantes*.

The book brought me a lot of hate mail. One letter was signed "God". I did not believe it was genuine. Surely he signs himself "God Almighty"– and not from a Bexhill address.

"Make Love Not War" was one of the saner slogans of the age. I still bore Heinlein's *Starship Troopers* in mind. The question of war was one I found hard to resolve. That war is terrible is a platitude; that the two world wars have done damage to Britain, and to generations unborn while they were waged, is indisputable. But for me personally the war came as a kind of saviour; it may have played hell with my morality, but it was a great character-builder. I had no character at all before 1939.

In *Cryptozoic*, there is a joke about the Tripeshop Troopers. Harry had a much better go at army-lovers in his classic of humour, *Bill, the Galactic Hero* (which he dedicated to me). It actually stopped at least one reader from joining up. Literature can change the world.

There's a fine moment in Woody Allen's film *Stardust Memories*, when Woody is surrounded by an audience hostile to his latest (serious) movie. He tries to explain how concerned he is with the state of everything. And a man says to him, "You want to do humanity a favour? Tell funnier jokes."

Bill made me resolve to allow more humour into my work. And to write – at last – directly about the war. And sex.

CHAPTER 13

Wandering Scholars

Ever since 1977, one of the miracles of technology, a probe called Voyager 2, has been working its way steadily from Earth, beaming back information on the outer planets of our solar system with about as much power as a firefly puts out. And we have gone about our own affairs.

Winds of 400 m.p.h. blow in the stratosphere of Neptune. Yet I talk about my own small concerns.

As Ann Radcliffe set her action in the Pyrenees and Mary Shelley hers in the Alps, so we — with as true an instinct – set our stories on untrodden planets. It seems to lend the happenings a little significance.

When I began writing, I had no idea that there existed an active science fiction fandom. These days, I belong to several organisations; the SF world loves to organise itself into societies. I am a founder member of the Science Fiction Writers of America, the only English member who joined at its inception at the invitation of the founder, Damon Knight. I am also Vice-President with Harry of the Birmingham SF Group, founded by Rog Peyton.

British fandom sought me out soon after my story appeared in the *Observer*. A letter arrived from a lady who worked in the picturesquely named Hanging Sword Passage. Her name was Helen Winnick and she was one of the formidable ladies who then helped to run London fandom. In no time, I was sitting in a London pub with the likes of Walter Gillings, John Brunner, Sam Youd ("John Christopher") and such visitors as C. S. Lewis.

I have mentioned the BSFA. The BSFA organises conventions. Conventions are big in the United States, and big business. The American ones scare me. I prefer the British cons, and have attended many of them all over the country.

To begin, my role at these events was a modest one, but I was encouraged to get on to the platform and speak on panels, to argue such crucial questions as "Can SF ever become literature?" ("Not while — is still writing it," called some wag in the audience.)

When the trembling stopped, I agreed to take solo spots. How soon, how easily, reticence turns to exhibitionism. An SF audience rates as one of the best in the world. It is friendly, well-informed, sharp, humorous, will not stand cant or rank being pulled on it. It knows the tribal customs. Having experienced convention audiences, one comes to see one's readership in the same terms.

There never was such a creative readership as the SF readership. The representatives one meets at conventions may contain a few nutcases, but by and large these are men and women who wish to write themselves, or will edit, or run their own fanzines, or are artists or critics. Most of today's editors and publishers – editor Malcolm Edwards at Grafton is an example – were fans. I met Malcolm first when he was up at Cambridge, running the flourishing SF club there.

It is a privilege for a writer to meet his audience, although he should refuse to be led by it and must defy it if it wars with his instincts – as I found to be the case in the late sixties. As Tarkovsky says, in the passage already quoted, you should not passively accept the tastes of your audience.

With confidence comes responsibility. I have had the honour and responsibility of being Guest of Honour at World Cons twice, on both occasions in England. Only John W.

Campbell and Robert Heinlein have fared as well.

Conventions in Japan and Europe are more of a challenge. It is important to accept if asked to be Guest of Honour, to my mind. What fortune to find that one's work is read and enjoyed by people of different races and creeds. I was delighted to learn that the Helliconia novels are available in *samizdat* in the Soviet Union, even if it puts not a single rouble in my pocket. Indeed, I now have a *samizdat* version on my shelves, as prized as an incunabulum. The countries that are of great interest are those of Eastern Europe; because they are less familiar than France and Germany and the other countries of the West. Hungary, Poland, Czechoslovakia, East Germany, Jugoslavia, have traditions like ours, and yet are different. It is educational and enjoyable to rub up against these differences.

A grey area exists for me between thought and action. Harry Harrison is a doer. When Harry went with his family to live in Ireland, he organised two splendid conventions in Dublin. At these conventions in the mid-seventies he founded, with a little help from his friends, World SF.

World SF has worked, on its modest scale. Our early supporters included Peter Kuczka of Hungary, Ion Hobana of Romania and Eremi Parnov of Russia, as well as such English friends as Christopher Priest. We got together and hobnobbed even in the era of Brezhnev and a gung-ho Ronald Reagan. We have flourishing chapters in Poland, Italy and Japan, with smaller groups scattered through the West European countries. In these post-*glasnost* days, more Russians can attend our conferences – for instance the 1988 meeting in Budapest, long to be remembered.

Harry was first President of World SF, to be followed subsequently by Frederik Pohl, me, Sam Lundwall, Gianfranco Viviani, and Norman Spinrad, in that order. Presidency means an extensive commitment of time and money; you have to be an idealist; but we do serve the cause of international amity as well as that of science fiction.

One of our stalwarts in World SF is Sam Lundwall, the

Swedish writer. Sam is a true international man, who has probably travelled more than anyone in World SF. He has organised conventions in Stockholm and Helsinki, speaks seven languages, is always full of wit and humour. Sam is famous as a singer, in which art he exerts such pulling power that he has used Abba as a backing group, for instance in his "King Kong Blues". Like me, Sam has written a history of science fiction; he also owns a publishing house, Delta, which publishes novels and the long-running *Jules Verne Magasinet*. He and I put together the *Penguin World Omnibus of SF* – a test of international friendship if ever there was one.

The SF and fantasy fields, when it comes to award-giving, work rather on the principle of the Caucus-race in *Alice*, as enunciated by the Dodo: "Everybody has won, and all must have prizes." The two chief awards are the Hugo, given by popular vote, and the Nebula, given by the vote of members of the Science Fiction Writers of America.

The SFWA has become far from exclusive lately – one fantasy story and you're in – but its awards still count for something in commercial if not literary terms. Records show that both Hugo and Nebula awards are given almost exclusively to American writers unless your name happens to be Arthur C. Clarke. Geography is to blame for this state of affairs rather than xenophobia: you have to be on the spot and do a little campaigning. World SF awards are different.

World SF awards are not given for fiction. The Karel Awards (named after Karel Čapek) – take the form of neat little glass statuettes. They go to translators, the people on whom we depend to freight novels from one language to another. It is a useful award, Fred Pohl's brainchild. Our other two major annual awards, which I instituted during my term of office, are the President's Award, for Independence of Thought, and the Harrison Award (named after our founder), for Improving the Status of SF Internationally. These take the form of translucent acrylic monoliths, blue for the President, shamrock green for the Harrison (after Harry's adopted homeland). They are truly international awards which have real meaning, and now repose in studies as far apart as Beijing, Nice, Reading, Vista and Buenos Aires.

There's honour in survival. Some of our members have survived we know not what under government policy in their countries. We are fortunate in England: we need nothing more than cash and curiosity and we can travel the world. On a global scale, it seems to be a rare liberty.

Following my first visit to the United States in 1965, I have been back there almost every year. It is difficult for an Englishman to think of the States as a foreign country – and, I trust, vice versa. One does not come across the sometimes self-defeating irony prevalent in Europe. The cast of thought is different.

I once flew down to Atlanta, Georgia, to stay with friends. Atlanta airport is vast and well organised. Bud Foote, noted scholar and wit, met me there.

As we were strolling towards his car, I noticed dozens of Boeing 747s decorated with the Delta insignia.

"Delta seems big hereabouts," I said.

"Yep," Bud agreed. "It started as a crop-spraying enterprise."

That sort of spirit is absent in Eastern Europe. In Eastern Europe, there are national airlines which would do well to shrink into crop-spraying enterprises. Communism has proved to be a disease, as those afflicted recognised; but it is a disease springing from capitalism.

Eastern Europe did not become what it is today – whatever it is – solely because Soviet tanks got there first in 1945. The rivers run the wrong way. Much of it is broken and mountainous country, particularly in the south and the rumpled lands of the Balkans. How beautiful the old Hapsburg territory was; the Hapsburgs imposed their own sort of order on the region – an order now looked back on by ageing Austrians, Slovenes, Czechs and Hungarians with some nostalgia.

In the north, of course, lies that flat North European plain, on which most of the Poles live. The plain has proved impossible to defend. Poles are unfortunate in their neighbours.

This is a Polish joke we heard some while ago in Poznan.

A Pole is walking in the fields. He has a gun. He meets a Russian and a German. So which does he shoot first?

Answer: He shoots the German first. Because – well, you know the old saying, Business before pleasure.

And there's past history. The shadow of the crescent moon of Turkey was once cast across much of Europe. When the Ottoman Empire was a great power in the world, the Muslim visitation encompassed the subcontinent as far as the gates of Austria, while the remains of the great Moorish occupation of Spain may still be visited in Cordoba, Granada and Seville.

What is now Jugoslavia was for centuries the resource from which the janissaries were drawn. There's a moving description of the marching away of Serbian children by Turkish guards, while their mothers, weeping, fall slowly behind the progress back to Istanbul, in the Nobel-prize-winning novel by Ivo Andrić, *The Bridge on the Drina (Na Drini Ćuprija)*. Christian Orthodox children were trained up to become the formidable fighting force of Islam.

When Kinglake spoke of leaving wheel-going Europe and entering the splendour and the havoc of the East, he was talking about exchanging one great system of faith for another.

And wherever you went in Eastern Europe for the last thirty years, from Hungary to Macedonia, your guides would stand you in churches to tell you terrible tales of bloodshed, as if the altar at which one should make one's peace with God was in fact a stage for slaughter and scimitar-play.

Ideology is a terrible scourge of the intellect. We are fortunate that women are more immune to it than men. Nationalism is almost as bad – and women catch that complaint as easily as men. Jingoism is as prevalent in England as in America. It will need to die for the future to remain habitable as populations increase. Johnson was right, as so often –

patriotism is the last refuge of a scoundrel. Unfortunately, in this respect, we are nearly all scoundrels.

Budapest is a powerful and exciting capital to visit. Yet if one wished to commit suicide, the Hungarian National Gallery would be a good place to choose. There on the walls of the upper gallery hang vast canvases depicting costumed slaughter, the dreadful past. What was it all about? Harrison's response comes back: "Don't ask." Horses lie dead on the heath. Intestines drip from battlements. The Banat fills with blood. Beturbaned heads roll. Dobozi clutches his wife as the horsemen thunder out from the pillaged city. Melancholy Queen Isabella says her last farewell to Transylvania.

In the well-ordered art galleries of the West, where the air-conditioning works, pamphlets are available in every chamber in three languages, and the restaurant next door is excellent – there hang the great crucifixions, blood dripping from wounds, Christ's grey body dragged down from Golgotha against a threatening sky, naked flesh being lacerated in various ways.

It's all at odds with our quiet English country churches, where ladies still do the flowers every week, where there are pleasingly melancholy smells of damp and decaying plaster instead of the reek of blood. Here, we still have parsons, at least for a little longer. *There*, you meet only guides, and the onion-domed chapels of the Kremlin are museums.

Westernisation has crept into Eastern Europe. But it is not the West – though, as I make a final revision of these pages, it shows every sign of wishing to be the West, and Estonia, Latvia and Lithuania link hands in hope. And when all we Europeans have ecus in our pockets, I daresay that dinars and zlotys and Czech crowns will still be unnegotiably around to remind us of the frontier, less definable than the Iron Curtain but more permanent, which historically divides Europe in two. Who knows? Recent events suggest that the Hungarian forint may soon become negotiable.

The building of civilisation is like the building of a city.

Time and tremendous human effort go into its making. Leningrad, once St Petersburg, stands as a brilliant example of difficulty and progress. It was constructed under orders from Peter the Great on impossible land taken from the Swedes. How many hundreds of peasants died in its construction? There were no Russian architects equal to the task in Peter's day: the city was designed by French and Italians. It was to be Russia's new capital, looking towards the West. It was a city – as all cities are to greater or lesser degree – to change minds.

We see Russia, and the Soviet Union of which Russia is the tail that wags the dog, as caught between Europe and Asia. I was once in Asia, in Japan, with a party of Russians. Together we explored the complexities of Tokyo. I was in no doubt on that occasion that Russians were Europeans.

In 1977, I spent a fortnight in the USSR, under the aegis of the Arts Council and Yevgeny Yevtushenko. Six of us went in a group, in rather privileged circumstances. We travelled in Russia and in Georgia, and were escorted every inch of the way. The hospitality was splendid. One of our escorts, Victor Pogorstin, recently visited us in Oxford with his wife and child. That could happen in 1989 and not before 1985.

With us on that trip was Elaine Feinstein, novelist, poet, translator of Russian poetry. Elaine has remained a friend of mine, and I recently had a public conversation with her in the ICA. My most vivid memory of Moscow is of Elaine managing to talk with a Soviet dissident on the platform at the railway station, where their conversation could not be bugged. Such was the miserable atmosphere in Moscow at that time. Although the Georgians have a reputation as scoundrels in Moscow, life in Tbilisi was more cheerful, the hidden pressures less unpleasant.

Our hosts were generous to us. We had been in Moscow only a day or two when the six of us were each presented with an envelope – a gift of pocket money to spend, we were told. Ninety-seven roubles each. Very nice. Thanks.

Two days later, another envelope, another ninety-seven roubles. Very nice. Thanks.

In Leningrad, the same. Another envelope, another ninety-seven roubles.

By then gratitude had abated sufficiently for us to say amongst ourselves, "Why this odd sum? Why not one hundred roubles?"

And to come up with the answer, "Someone is getting a little cut on every envelope."

We flew south, over the snaggle-toothed Caucasus. In Tbilisi, the envelopes came round again. Very nice. Thanks. This time, they contained ninety-three roubles.

An opportunity came in 1979 to visit the other great Communist power, the People's Republic of China. The country was then the world's flavour-of-the-month – as it remained for many a year. Chairman Hua was in temporary control before Deng Xiaoping took over the reins. Chairman Mao still lay in state in the great Hall of the People in Tiananmen Square.

I formed one of a group of six Distinguished Persons, so called, to whom *Life in the West* is dedicated.

We flew by Pakistan Airlines from Rawalpindi – Islamabad – at dawn one October day, right over that wondrous terrain which surely must remind even the most frivolous-minded of mortality, the Himalayas. For two hours the Boeing winged over the mountainous white Roof of the World. Photography was forbidden as we entered Chinese air space.

Far, far below, a guard hut stood, iced up by a frozen river, between two great snow-covered blades of mountain. Nothing moved. Some poor bastard was down there on guard duty.

Slogan at Peking (Beijing) airport, prominent in Chinese calligraphy and English:
WE HAVE FRIENDS ALL OVER THE WORLD

We were possessed by China. We longed to decode its

secrets. Because those secrets appeared embedded openly in the calligraphy which confronts one everywhere, this seemed possible. So even after a long day of travel and touring machine factories, of production brigades and lectures, we would summon to our various hotels in the evening journalists, trade unionists, academics, anyone who would come, to question them or answer their questions.

At other times, we questioned each other. Felix Greene, because of his long association with China, was of especial interest. Felix, "Friend of China", led our delegation until he had to go into hospital. He was a saintly character, with sharp eyes, spare, confident yet never arrogant, amusing, knowledgeable, willing to listen. We asked him one evening what had converted him to socialism.

I was made aware of the injustices in our social system very early, as a small boy. I woke up on Christmas morning and tiptoed downstairs before any of the family were awake. My favourite maid, Anne, was laying the fire in the drawing-room, where our Christmas tree stood, brightly decorated. Presents were piled round the room. I ran up to Anne where she was kneeling at the grate, put my arms round her, and wished her a merry Christmas.

"Oh, Christmas isn't for the likes of us, Master Felix," she said.

Iris Murdoch and I were invited to address a gathering of Chinese literary figures at the Friendship Association in Peking. Iris is a brilliant talker and delivered an extempore summary of the state of affairs in British philosophy. I spoke on science and the imagination, and the legend of Frankenstein, bearing in mind Hazlitt's definition of genius or originality as a strong mental quality, which brings out a new quality in nature.

Our audience was silent at first. Then someone spoke up and said the interpreter should be dismissed: they understood us better without his interventions. It then emerged that most of them spoke excellent English. The proceedings became less formal, developing into a general conversation, aided by the ready Chinese sense of humour. The man sitting opposite me across the table had a rugged countenance. I had observed him with interest, and saw he was scrutinising me. Eventually, he passed a note over to me, saying, "It happens I am translating one of your stories into Chinese for the magazine I edit, *World Literature*. It is a good surprise to find you in Peking. Perhaps we can have a talk afterwards." So I met Wang Fengzhen, who became the first member of World SF in China.

Felix Greene underwent an operation for cancer while we were in China. While the rest of the VIPs waited in Peking for an audience with the leader, I flew to Shanghai. I presented books to the university and stayed with Philip Smith II and his wife Susan, who were teaching English through SF. The devotion of the "foreign specialists", as they were called, to the Chinese was touching. It was impossible not to love the students, or not to be exasperated by the bureaucracy that hemmed them in. Their morals were more than Victorian. No sex life had been detected by the foreign specialists, despite plentiful research into the subject. When I lectured in a classroom, under two great portraits of Chairmen Mao and Hua, people struggled at the bars of the windows to get in. In English classrooms they do the reverse.

We were eventually granted audience with Deng Xiaoping himself. He was small and smoked, and kept a tin spittoon under his chair. "I'm a peasant," he said. A camera crew from Hong Kong, paid for out of Felix's pocket, photographed us asking Deng questions. I asked him about Chinese intentions regarding space.

I forget what he replied.

It doesn't matter what he said. In 1989, we witnessed scenes in the heart of Peking, in Tiananmen Square, where

Chinese people were shot down with Chinese bullets by the Chinese army.

Somewhere I have a photo of me shaking hands with Deng Xiaoping. We look very pleased to meet each other.

He didn't use the spittoon.

In the light of recent events, one of Deng's replies was ominous. He was asked a question, I believe by Iris, concerning individual freedom.

He replied that, yes, there was individual freedom, of course, although it was being abused by young people, who threatened to bring back anarchy. Pressed to amplify his response, Deng said that an example of individual liberty would be the production unit, which was free to set its own targets of output, its crops, its standards of education and so on.

In other words, he could not distinguish between individual and corporate freedom. This is a problem the gerontocracy of China still has to overcome.

In the China we saw, no one seemed to work. Streets were always full of people strolling. When we entered any workshop or factory, the workers knocked off, lit up cigarettes and watched us. Peasants in the fields leaned on their hoes. The pace everywhere was slow. Country roads were dotted with families joy-riding on tractors. We heard that tractors were so new and precious they were not to be spoiled by being driven on the fields. It made sense.

One of our numbers, hot in quest of Truth, asked the peasants we met in the production brigades, "Are you happy in China? Are you really happy?"

The answer was always, "Yes".

But if you have no standards of comparison?

Would you rather be in Philadelphia?

And how do you get there from Feng Huo No. 1 Production Brigade?

*   *   *

142

The production brigades were more enjoyable than their names suggested. Before leaving England, we had been briefed by serious young men at SACU on their organisation and rates of productivity, etc. It had sounded very portentous.

The reality was different – at least as we were allowed to experience it. One brigade near Kunming was run by Ye, a non-Han minority group which had in the past experienced "big nation chauvinism", (i.e. persecution). The farmers were jolly and red-faced. The October day was mild. We sat about on benches in the open while fruit – tasty persimmons – and enormous vacuum flasks of tea were set before us by women in tribal dress. They threshed corn prettily.

We saw what we were intended to see.

And how idyllic it looked, how romantic the rolling stretches of Chinese landscape.

At that place, outside one homestead, was a circular concrete sty in which a porker lived out its innocent life. In the middle of the sty stood a pillar supporting a circular platform. The platform was sheltered by a concrete umbrella. It had a circular hole in its floor. You climbed to the platform up a spiral concrete stair.

This was the toilet. The family emptied its bowels through the hole early in the morning. The pig – aptly referred to by Mao as "the shit factory" – received the droppings gratefully, and grew fat for New Year.

Not as revolting as it might sound. Hygienic and economical – and, after all, these country people were perforce almost vegetarian, living on rice, grain and cabbage.

Being in China was the nearest one could get to visiting another populous planet.

Do visitors from the West experience China as beautiful or ugly? Both beauty and ugliness exist there, just as elsewhere. As science and experience teach, objective and subjective are not to be separated: what one sees is what one can see. To me, who had dreamed of China ever since he was a boy, magic was everywhere. An old fence, silvered with age, was not just an old fence. It was a Chinese old fence.

Yet Peking was brutal. Much of it dated from the fifties and the time of Sino-Soviet accord, so that the disastrous evidences of Stalinism lie heavy over the centre.

Although the people are kind and tolerant and witty, their script is written by a Kafkaesque government. Nothing is what it seems. A man will make a remark to you in Xian which you consider striking, subversive and original. You fly to Kunming, miles and provinces away. There another man will say exactly the same thing. Here are reflections. Where is truth?

All the institutions which controlled our activities were powerful yet nebulous. I made determined attempts while in Peking to visit a publishing house. My lobbying succeeded up to a point. Two gentlemen, humorous, well-informed, came from the People's Literature Publishing House and talked to me in my room for two hours. I never saw their establishment. All is shadowy. Only the Party is real.

When I walked on the Great Wall, I found myself thinking of Richard Nixon. He was the one who had the sense to get on the phone to Mao Tse-tung, after years of hostile silence. When my wife went on the Wall, she approached it by donkey, up an unmade road.

In Boswell's *Life of Johnson*, Boswell reports Johnson's typically individual view of the Great Wall. Saying he wished to see it for himself, Johnson added, "You would do what would be of importance in raising your children to eminence . . . They would be at all times regarded as the children of a man who had gone to view the wall of China. I am serious, sir."

Our children, I believe, do not take this view.

Critic in a Jacuzzi

Serbo-Croat has two words for dying, one referring to human death, one to animal death, although two animals are the exception to the rule. Bees and dolphins are irregular, and take the human form of the verb.

Similarly, the English language has two nouns for fiction, fiction and science fiction. The latter is not quite human.

Writers of science fiction can look after themselves, and many of them prosper. No institution looms over them. They can take a romantic view of themselves, seeing themselves as the *steppenwulfs* of society.

No such recourse is open to the scholars – mainly an American breed – who teach or study science fiction. They are scattered. Their institutions often oppress them. SF writers often oppose them.

My sympathies are with the scholars.

The battleground on which I have fought is not merely the divide between fiction and SF, between human and animal. It is also across another – perhaps equally fictitious – divide, that between creation and criticism.

Our characters have to encompass struggles with conflicting kinds of belief. Mary Shelley's father, William Godwin, is generally seen as a cold, unloving father. So he was. But he had a miserable childhood in Wisbech, of all places, was often

145

whipped, and was brought up in a strict Calvinist faith, believing in hell-fire; he trained to be a preacher. Doubt entered when he read a French book of the Enlightenment. Those two warring systems of thought, based on faith and reason, also penetrated the sad heart of his daughter Mary and, *mutatis mutandis,* still bedevil us today.

Do you imagine that space travel will resolve the struggle?

Over the years, people turned to me to do things for them and on the whole I did them. The grasshopper attempted to become an ant. A staff shortage always existed in the ranks of SF.

So between the work taken seriously, the writing of short stories and novels, came other tasks – lecturing, campaigning, writing many letters. I filled several managerial posts, often in association with Harry. He and I edited a *Year's Best SF* series for a decade, Harry doing all the donkey work; I provided Afterwords.

Here I am again in 1990, doing the same job for a new annual series, the Orbit *SF Yearbook*, which David S. Garnett edits. David is amusing, a pleasure to work for, the task is engaging.

Harry and I also edited a line of classic reprints, the SF Master series. Long and hard we fought for that series, and managed to bring into print several excellent neglected novels, such as Philip K. Dick's *Martian Timeslip* and Joseph O'Neill's *Land Under England,* as well as several foreign novels. The series appeared in hardcover and paperback.

We also edited a brave book entitled *Hell's Cartographers* (a bow in the direction of our friend Kingsley Amis). *Hell's Cartographers* contains memoirs by six leading writers. It was a new thing. It started a trend. Two of our authors, Damon Knight and Frederik Pohl, found that this autobiographical mode was agreeable and went on to write books in the same vein. Our youngest author was Robert Silverberg. His revelation of how he worked – and prospered by it – remains of tremendous interest to anyone who wishes to understand the American SF world.

With a publisher/packager called Trewin Copplestone, I compiled *SF Art*, a large-size volume packed with illustrations in black and white and colour from the old magazines. It ranked artists according to name for the first time, allowing them a little of the dignity rightfully theirs.

During the eighties, SF and SF art ceased to be a secret movement and became professional, but early covers and illustrations hold great charm and humour. Will they ever be exhibited alongside Max Ernst and Matta, I wonder?

Anyone who has visited an exhibition of original Patrick Woodroffe paintings must wonder if a new Bosch is in our midst, to be hailed as such only after his death.

Following the success of the Penguin anthologies, I edited many anthologies of other people's work, too numerous to mention. One series I put together for Anthony Cheetham. Anthony must rank among the most successful of British publishers. He bought *Hothouse* for paperback when he first entered publishing, and has managed to publish something or other of mine in almost every company for which he has worked or has owned. Our most successful anthology is *Galactic Empires*.

For the anthologies I wrote introductions and commentaries. So I discovered myself to be a critic as well as a story teller. Somehow, critical volumes accrued, of which *Billion Year Spree* is the most measured example. *Billion* was in part a proselytising exercise. I did not wish greatly to be associated with the kind of writing then being lauded, which appeared in the pages of magazines associated with Hugo Gernsback, the "Planet of Mad Atavism" kind of story.

Some of the best English writers follow the tradition of criticism with fiction. Christopher Priest is a good example, although he has produced too little criticism besides his own individual, vibrantly nervous fiction. He has been widely influential in the field, for instance on Robert Holdstock, who edits original anthologies with Chris Evans. Holdstock is also author of the brilliant *Mythago Wood*, perhaps the most rich and deep novel of the eighties, despite competition from the likes of Garry Kilworth, Iain Banks, Bob Shaw, Tanith Lee, Terry Pratchett, Paul McAuley, and other British writers.

When that new breed, American scholars, presented me with the Pilgrim Award for criticism, it was not left on a doorstep, like the Hugo. Instead, I flew out to Iowa to receive it from the hands of Arthur O. Lewis. That award is one to treasure. The scholars did not know me personally, nor I them.

The number of men and women who taught SF/fantasy in colleges and universities was then, in 1978, on the increase. I had predicted their rise in *Billion Year Spree*.

The inbred quality of science fiction is slow to disperse. It accounts for the anger which greets any divergence from tribal creeds within the ranks – as with the New Wave movement in the sixties or the Cyberpunk writers of the eighties.

The scholars in the main did not come from fandom but from academia. They formed themselves into the SFRA, the Science Fiction Research Association. It was the SFRA which awarded me the Pilgrim for *Billion Year Spree* and other "distinguished contributions to the study of science fiction". It was the SFRA which encouraged me to take part in the scholarly aspect of affairs.

SF should be taught and examined critically; such attention represents a natural expansion of the field.

Since the Pilgrim, I have collected more critical awards than any other SF writer. I am the sole holder of the James Blish Award for Excellence in Science Fiction Criticism – an award commemorating my old friend, Blish. The award I most value is the first IAFA Distinguished Scholarship Award for Outstanding Contributions to the History and Criticism of the Fantastic in Literature. It was presented to me in Houston, Texas, in 1986.

The IAFA, the International Association for the Fantastic in the Arts, was founded in the early eighties by Dr Robert A. Collins, a genial and scholarly man in the Humanities Division of Florida Atlantic University. Bob Collins began to hold annual conferences in Boca Raton, Florida, in 1979. I was invited to the 1981 meeting and have been going ever since, wherever the conference has been held – either in Florida or Texas.

The IAFA conferences have been a source of great enjoyment and inspiration. The scholars have many problems within academia, encountering the same sort of prejudice as the writers. Those prejudices will slowly be overcome.

When I first flew over to Boca Raton, I felt my reputation to be at a low ebb. The friendly way in which the IAFA received me is not forgotten. The academics work hard, but are prepared to break off for horseplay in the evening. For two years, I taught writing during their conferences with such great names in the field as James Gunn – remarkable both as writer and teacher – and Theodore Sturgeon.

At that period, I was suffering from the first onslaught of what was later diagnosed as Post-Viral Fatigue Syndrome, known in the States as Epstein Barr Syndrome, and trying to conceal the fact. It was almost impossible to stay awake while reading the piles of manuscripts submitted by students. Yet the informality of Boca Raton and the pleasure of sitting chatting to those adult students in the cheapest café in the vicinity remains with me.

As most writers need sub-editing, so most need criticism. It is natural to feel intense curiosity about what others make of your work. Reviewers write in haste, but criticism is more deeply considered.

One of the challenges of IAFA conferences is to be present when critics read papers on one's own work: a luxury cast in the terror mode, particularly when Charles Platt is the critic. It must be as teasing for the critic as for the author. I recall sitting near Ursula LeGuin when one of the most erudite of critics, Darko Suvin, was delivering a eulogy from the platform on her novel, *The Dispossessed*. LeGuin's expression, as I interpreted it, was one of dismay. One readily understood how she felt.

Nicholas Ruddick, of the University of Regina in Canada, is one of the critics at IAFA meetings. He delivered a paper on my writing, "Brood of Mary", in Houston. It's amusing and often perceptive, not least because it understands the complexity underlying the simplicity of a writer's thought; it shows an affection for obscurity of which I have never entirely rid myself.

"Brood of Mary" is presented here as an appendix.

In Boca Raton days, some of the funding for the conference came from Mrs Burnett Swan, whose son, a fantasy writer, Thomas Burnett Swan, had been an alumnus of the Florida Atlantic University. Mrs Swan was a grand lady, advanced in years but still capable of enjoying an occasion. She lived, it was rumoured, in a vast mansion in the north of the state where, if money was needed, she sold the odd painting or suit of armour. I imagined her as the last of the cotton millionairesses, and hope it was so.

On one occasion I was deputed to escort Mrs Swan to the banquet. We rode in a magnificent car, all mahogany and red plush within, like a San Francisco bordello in 1899, if movies are to be believed. Her chauffeur was a large dignified black man in uniform.

"Are we going the right way, James?"

"I thought you would prefer this route, Mrs Swan, it being more picturesque."

"Thank you, James."

"And I took the liberty of bringing along your shawl, Mrs Swan, case you were cold later."

"Very thoughtful of you, James."

It was all immensely gothic. She loved the banquet and was entertaining company.

Two remarkable men became presidents of the newly

formed IAFA, Roger Schlobin, followed by Marshall Tymn. Between them, they gathered a small group of scholars who proved excellent organisers. Several of them belong to both IAFA and SFRA. It is important there should be no more than friendly rivalry between the two bodies.

I first met Marshall Tymn in Idaho, in 1978, when his businesslike way of taking a class impressed me. Later, he escorted a group of student teachers to England. When I persuaded him to bring them to Oxford, he came down with his wife Darlene and twenty student teachers. We did a walking tour of places where writers with connections with the SF/fantasy field had worked: Lewis Carroll, Max Beerbohm, Aldous Huxley, Oscar Wilde, Charles Williams, C. S. Lewis and J. R. R. Tolkien. To stand in Tolkien's rooms was almost too much for some of them.

After the tour, they all came back to Orchard House, where Margaret served a splendid buffet lunch and the students found how strong British beer was.

I lectured to them with the assistance of Dr Willis McNelly, a lively academic from Fullerton, California, who happened to be staying with us at the time.

Although we were grateful for the patronage extended by Mrs Swan, the IAFA had to decide to be self-supporting. Thanks to the energies of all concerned, and the needs of scholars, it quickly became so. Under Marshall's leadership, the association has grown into a great catalytic force, an annual inspiration.

Marshall Tymn has now retired from the presidency of the IAFA, the position being taken over by Donald Palumbo, yet another witty scholar.

During the course of our recent conference in Fort Lauderdale, the tenth, over one hundred papers were delivered on a wide range of topics. There were readings by guest writers, panels, exhibitions of fantastic masks, a room of scholarly books difficult to obtain outside the USA, and many other items: a very full programme. I have been allotted a privileged role as the IAFA's Special Permanent Guest, and was able to repay this kindness by securing Doris Lessing as the conference's Guest of Honour.

Lessing, in her books and in person, reminds us of things that we need always to be told concerning goodness, modesty and wit. Sharing a jacuzzi with Doris Lessing represents the peak of my somewhat obscure literary career.

CHAPTER 15

Stubbs Soldiers On

The shadow of necessity, the spectre of poverty, is never far from us. Poverty was all about when I was a boy – not just in East Dereham, Norfolk, where I was brought up, but in the country in general, and in Wales and Scotland.

Poverty is no invention of the eighties, as some seem to imagine. The unemployed, the people thrown on the scrap heap, the people who never had a chance, the ones who could never make it: they form the silent multitudes of history. Wretched grinding hardship has been the lot of most English people (useless here to speak of the rest of the world) throughout the centuries.

As a boy, I felt a strong bond with two artists who emerged from poverty: Gracie Fields, who came from a poor Lancashire cotton town, Rochdale, and Charlie Chaplin, who was born in a London slum, Whitechapel. Both escaped from their origins to brighter climes by dint of talent and hard work, Gracie – "Our Gracie" – to Anacapri, Charlie to California (though not for keeps). In their time, in the days before TV and the publicity machines which throw up pop stars, both Gracie and Charlie were loved with passion and famed beyond belief. When Gracie fell ill just before the war, she received two million letters of sympathy. The population of England was then about forty million.

153

As for Charlie . . . the cinema in Dereham, the Exchange Theatre, so called because it had just recently ceased to be a corn exchange, had only to put its life-size cardboard figure of the little tramp with that runagate smile outside its doors, and a queue would form before it. Both Charlie and Gracie mixed pathos with humour. It made them more than two-dimensional figures.

Comedians generally hail from nowhere. Few dukes take to the boards. I believe that Max Miller, "The Cheekie Chappie", was illegitimate. And then there were Flanagan and Allen, with their haunting down-and-out songs, their star turn being "Underneath the Arches".

When I became a Faber author, I was moved by a book entitled *The Boy Down Kitchener Street*, written by Leslie Paul. I met Leslie Paul. He told me he had made it all up, but it was the sort of childhood he dreamed of . . .

I have often puzzled over that remark. But after all, most fiction is about experience: experience lived through, longed for, or dreaded – and sometimes all three at once, for boundaries between reality and imagination are less clear than we like to pretend. Were it not so there would be no literature: we have lived more intensely because we have read Dostoevsky and Dickens and Dick.

My attempts to write about humble life have been many, and mostly confined to science fiction. In the late sixties, however, I saw a chance to combine this desire with a description of my experiences in the army.

Coming out of the army, settling in Barnstaple, Devon, I spent some of my demob leave trying to write a novel. This was the doomed "Hunter Leaves the Herd". The exercise came to grief for three reasons, firstly because I could not sufficiently detach myself from the need to discover what England was like, secondly because I was ill-equipped to write a novel, and thirdly because the censorship laws did not at that time permit one to present any reasonable facsimile of how soldiers actually spoke and behaved.

Eric Linklater circumvented the latter problem in his novel *Private Angelo,* and added to the comedy by having his troops say "shocking" instead of "fucking". It was "the shocking army this" and "the shocking army that".

In 1960 came the trial of D. H. Lawrence's novel, *Lady Chatterley's Lover,* on the grounds of obscenity. A remarkable cultural event. Historians have seen the acquittal of the novel as the opening shot of the more liberal sixties. Certainly, from then on language was to be freer. With the arrival of the Pill, sexual relationships also became freer; skirts did not go up to mini-length for nothing: they simplified the act of getting down to business for both sexes.

The fashion now is to denigrate the sixties. Yet the spirit at the time was in some ways hopeful and beautiful. That long dream of British Empire, sustained in its dead days by the grandiose dreams of Winston Churchill, was at last over; the Romans were becoming Italians. Relationships between people, between sexes and classes, were better or, at the least, more amenable to reconsideration. As there was greater freedom to travel, and greater energy in the arts, so there was greater sexual freedom.

The Horatio Stubbs saga is about a young man redeemed by the love of a bad woman – well, several bad women, to be honest. In his schooldays, Stubbs speaks up for masturbation, an aspect of sex not widely aired in the sixties; hence the significance of the title of the first book in the series, *The Hand-Reared Boy.* We leave him when war is about to break out. In the following volumes, *A Soldier Erect* and *A Rude Awakening,* Stubbs is in the army, at first in action in India and Burma and then, in the post-war period, as part of the army of occupation in Sumatra, in what had already become the Indonesian Republic.

Stubbs and his companions are downtrodden: soldiers, but victims of the war just as much as the whores they meet. I put a lot of humour into the books — humour goes with terrible times – and often laughed and wept over my typewriter, particularly when writing *A Rude Awakening*, where everyone has to bow to the great storm that had shaken the world. The East, even more conclusively than the West, was never going to be the same again.

My early intention was to write the whole Stubbs epic in one long narrative. However, I saw at the end of the first episode what an interesting shape it had, a curve somewhat like a boomerang. It should stand alone.

At that period, I acquired a new English agent, Hilary Rubinstein, who had recently bought the literary agency, A. P. Watt, the oldest in the business. Hilary put high-octane fuel into the engine of my sales. Working in his foreign department was Maggie Noach, later to start a literary agency of her own, who wrought marvels for my overseas business.

One of the first steps Hilary took was to wean me from Faber & Faber. I needed a lot of persuading. It was Faber who had approached me, and Charles Monteith had been such a genial publisher. However, reasons were presented to me for making the move, and so I did. It was while I was working on *Barefoot in the Head* that I wrote the piece which became *Hand-Reared Boy*.

"This is driving me crazy," I said to my wife, looking up from *Barefoot*. "I am beginning to see the New Animal out of the corner of my eye."

"Take a break and write something quite different," she said.

So I wrote *Hand-Reared Boy* before continuing to work on what I considered the more important project, *Barefoot*.

Hilary was an enthusiast for *HRB*. He sent it to publisher after publisher. It was too outspoken for many of them. In some houses – at Gollancz, for instance – it caused a board-room battle, with Giles Gordon on the side of what we regarded as enlightenment.

Eventually, the typescript arrived at Hutchinson, then presided over by Robert Lusty. It was accepted and was guided through the publishing processes by a young editor, Michael

Dempsey, an enthusiast for literature and alcohol.

Mike rang me one day. There were in-house problems about the foul language of the novel. He said, "Is there to be a follow-up to this?"

"Oh, yes."

" . . . It won't be as bad as this, will it?"

"Much worse. Stubbs will be in the army."

Mike's caution – so unlike him – revealed that trouble was coming.

Page proofs of the novel arrived on the desk of Robert Lusty just after Mike sent me a five-colour proof of the jacket. Lusty read the proofs and came rushing red-faced from his office.

"We can't publish this. It's pornography. I couldn't defend this in court."

Hutchinson threw the novel out. Sir Robert Lusty, as he now is, has a different version of events in his autobiography, *Bound to be Read*. Remembering exactly what happened is certainly a difficult art. But I did not take away my book as Lusty claims; I sued him for breaking contract.

I have often wondered: was he surprised to learn that adolescents masturbate?

The Times reported the story, with my photograph. Within forty-eight hours *HRB* had been bought by Tony Godwin, who had moved from Penguin to become the whizz-kid at Weidenfeld & Nicolson. Tony was a lively man, argumentative and original. In 1973, he gave me an advance of £5,000 to go out to India and write a book on the British Raj; when I realised I would have to learn to write and read Hindi, I returned the money. I admired Tony's impulsive nature.

So *HRB* came to rest with an energetic publisher, after it had been rejected by thirteen others – including, originally, Weidenfeld & Nicolson. This good fortune was owed to Hilary Rubinstein, who had faith in the novel, and persisted.

Choosing an agent is worse than choosing a publisher. After terrible tussles with a New York agent, I found myself looking again for someone to represent me in the States. Again the redoubtable Giles Gordon was involved. I happened to bump into him on a train, and we talked about the problem.

"I've got a good American agent in my office this morning, as it happens. Come and talk to her and see if you think she'll do."

So I went, rather wondering what questions to ask.

I need not have worried. In Giles's office was a smart, scrubbed Robin Straus. She asked me the questions.

She had never heard of me. She did not read science fiction. She would want to know what sort of standard my writing came up to before she took me on. It was a demanding interview.

I was much amused. This was the agent I wanted. I posted her a couple of my books. Fortunately, they passed the fitness test, and I was permitted to join what became the Robin Straus Literary Agency. And what began as business has developed into friendship.

HRB emerged under the Weidenfeld imprint in 1970, and for a brief while I was famous. Most of the London literary world had already read it, thanks to Mike Dempsey's judicious distribution of Hutchinson proof copies. This was to prove the only time I saw members of the great British public reading one of my hardcover books. It was a light book, only 45,000 words long, and it sailed like a kite to the top of the best-seller lists. Week by week I watched it there, and saw another book with a dull title creeping up on it. What on earth, I wondered, might *The Godfather* be about? But *The Godfather* soon rose to the top of the list, and swept my offering away.

As everyone knows, *The Godfather* was filmed by Francis Ford Coppola. Later, came *Godfather II*. There was no movie of *Hand-Reared Boy*. However, John Osborne attempted to make a film of it, with Jill Bennett as the school nursing sister, Virginia Traven, and Lindsay Anderson directing. The censor said there was no way in which scenes of masturbation could be shown. Men tortured to death, shot, decapitated, burnt, strangled, yes; but not, for heaven's sake, boys tossing themselves off.

It would be difficult for anyone who was not alive in the nineteen-thirties, to go no further back, to realise the hypocrisy with which sex was treated. That hypocrisy extended into the war period until, like England itself, it lost its power there.

As *Hand-Reared Boy* spoke out against such repressive attitudes, so did the continuation of the story, *A Soldier Erect*, which appeared in 1971. Stubbs by this time is in the army, is shipped out to India and fights the Japanese at the Battle of Kohima. The novel ends with the survivors of that horrendous bit of mayhem lying in their *charpoys*. There are no women in Burma with which to celebrate life. Every manjack has his hand on his cock. After all, on the morrow they move against Viswema.

In my mind, the sexual hypocrisy in the Far Eastern theatre of war, the one I knew, was linked to the contemptuous way the other ranks were treated. We were B.O.R.s, British Other Ranks, scarcely human, to be treated, when not fighting, like children. Out of sight, out of mind. Silence best policy, etc. There was a reputedly notorious restaurant in Bombay for officers only, which bore on its entrance the sign "No Indians, B.O.R.s, or Dogs". Perhaps it was as apocryphal as notorious; it was not unrepresentative.

Unlike World War I, the second war was fought in a just cause. Hitler was bent on war and the Japanese attacked Pearl Harbor, although we see with hindsight a certain inevitability about both German and Japanese moves. Hitler's racism, which led to the extermination of millions of Jews – and gypsies and Slavs and other races — has long been a subject for the world's disgust and dismay. But all the colonial powers were racist; their poisons were discharged into their colonies, rather than into Europe. It was OK to fuck Indian women, but you didn't bring 'em into the Mess.

The British were not the worst by a long chalk. Mahatma

159

Gandhi would have stood little chance of carrying out peaceful resistance under French or Dutch colonial rule. The British gave him the advantage of their inclinations, or at least their indecision.

Years later, I walked into Raffles Hotel arm-in-arm with a Singhalese lady. During the war for democracy, both of us would have been kicked out.

Soldier Erect is the only novel to treat the Burmese theatre of war from an underdog man-in-the-ranks point of view. One day, a couple of years ago, I switched on my radio to listen to the BBC and heard a general, possibly John Hackett, say, "Aldiss's *Soldier Erect* is the finest, frankest novel there is about the British serving man at war." I glowed. Christopher Priest said it was my best novel.

In his definitive book, *Wartime*, Paul Fussell calls my Stubbs trilogy "the most clear-sighted view, necessarily comic, of the pressure engendered by sexual deprivation in a bizarre context of male bonding with a vengeance. If one enemy was the Japanese, others almost as destructive were chastity, puritanism, repression, and hypocrisy."

As with *Hand-Reared Boy, Soldier Erect* was discussed as film material. At first, prospects looked hopeful. There were many dollars stowed away in India which could be tapped by companies wishing to film there. As we went further into the matter, it turned out that I was dealing with a company which could not get access to these multiple dollars.

"Couldn't you film it in Jugoslavia? Parts of it might pass as Burma," I enquired.

"If you could rewrite it, we could film it in Spain. Spain's as cheap as Jugoslavia now. Spain could stand in for bits of Germany."

"How do you mean, *Germany*?"

"If you could rewrite it so it's set in Germany instead of Burma . . . "

"But that's a whole different experience. The point about *Soldier Erect* is that it's about the Fourteenth Army and the war

160

in Burma."

"Yes, but if you rewrote it and made it the war in Germany. You know, early nineteen forty-five kind of thing."

This was an opportunity I failed to seize. Since then, Stanley Kubrick has shown us how, in *Full Metal Jacket*, the Vietnam war may be convincingly filmed in London's East End, given a few imported palm trees.

The Stubbs novels, being very English, did not travel so well abroad. They were, and they remain, popular in England. I saw them sold in porn shops in Praed Street, in yellow cellophane wrappers. To my mind, they are the opposite of harmful, their shocks salutary.

As a result of these two Stubbs novels, a kind of immortality is bestowed on me in the pages of the Supplement to the *Oxford English Dictionary*, and subsequently in the new edition of the *OED*, where I am quoted more than one hundred times, often as supplying an example of the troops' simple argot of World War II. Not to mention "crispy", "infrasound", "mepacrine", "oojah", "pressel", "sten", "videotape", and – best of all – "world".

Perhaps it was success. I lost my sense of direction. The reception of *Probability A* and *Barefoot* by the SF community was so hostile that I was reluctant to return to those chilly waters. *New Worlds* had collapsed. I did some anthologies. I buzzed about. Hepatitis came and went like a visiting comet. In 1973, Hilary Rubinstein said something to me about the terrible rate of inflation.

"What inflation?" I asked.

Then I recalled vaguely that the price of whisky was going up with every bottle I bought.

A correspondent writing to the *TLS* some time ago complained about a certain discretion in the *Dictionary of National Biography*. He said that while frankness about the sex lives of the biographees had improved, there was still unnecessary reticence about the effect of alcohol, often devastating, upon men's (chiefly men's) lives.

If this is hypocritical, it is a widely shared form of hypocrisy. Writers drink heavily, sometimes ostentatiously, sometimes secretly. And not only writers.

In 1972, Weidenfeld published my history of science fiction, *Billion Year Spree*. It represented a massive feat of reading. It was received with hostility by many sections of the SF field. My thought was that perhaps it might serve as a farewell to a sort of literature I had long enjoyed.

Billion contains a good argument. It seeks to rebut the notions of those who claim that science fiction is as old as Homer, or at least Lucian of Samosata in the second century AD. (Lucian's *True History* is a well-known satire on a lunar voyage.) It also rebuts claims that SF all began in a 25 cent pulp magazine which saw publication in 1926. Hard though it is to credit now, both these claims were seriously advanced – often by the same critic!

Both notions were absurd. One claimed too much, one too little. In comparison with *The Odyssey*, most SF, and indeed most other novels, are dwarfed. The stories in *Amazing*, when they were not reprints of earlier Verne and Wells short stories, were puerile. I had sampled *Amazing* as a boy and been fatigued by the poverty of style and imagination even then.

Moody though the reception of *Billion* was by the fans, it fell on fertile ground. It was picked up and read by Stanley Kubrick, who found himself described as "the great SF writer of the age", on the strength of *2001, Clockwork Orange* and *Dr Strangelove*. Kubrick got in touch with me, and later bought my short story "Super-Toys Last All Summer Long" for a movie. I worked with him for a while and greatly admire his creativity, although the film has still to appear. We still have hopes.

In Germany, Michael Görden also read *Billion*. He knew nothing about science fiction at the time, and had read none. *Billion* converted him into an enthusiast. He gained the post of editor with the firm of Bastei Lübbe and founded their SF list, which opened with Michael's own translation of *Billion*. Later, Bastei Lübbe threw a tremendous cultural party in Bergisch

Gladbach, near Cologne, to celebrate the success of their list.

David Wingrove also had read no science fiction until he chanced on *Billion*. He stalked me cautiously for a while until, finding me reasonably harmless, we became friends. Later, with Brian Griffin, he wrote a long volume called *Apertures* (1984), to try to explain what I was talking about. It is the best guide to my writing so far, published only in the USA.

When it became time to update *Billion* – in a volume that we christened *Trillion Year Spree* – David was a natural choice as my collaborator. He was younger, more enthusiastic, more energetic, and had read all the newer authors I neglected. Since then David has gone on to greater things. His mighty *Chung Kuo* in seven volumes will be one of the startlements of the nineties.

We had a little problem with the typescript of *Trillion*. Our contract was with Weidenfeld, who had published the original *Billion*, and for – if memory serves – eighty-five thousand words. Our typescript came to about one hundred and twenty-five thousand words. Weidenfeld's reception was very cool. A letter came from them saying that they could publish only if a co-publisher was found in New York, to share costs, and that the cheque they enclosed must be returned if this condition was not met.

Next, I heard from a lady appointed to be my editor. She knew little about science fiction, but she had her ideas about literature. What she said was that my paragraphs were too short for such a long book. My paragraphs! – the building blocks of a book, and carefully tended!

It was the end of a beautiful friendship. David and I returned the cheque. Weidenfeld agreed amiably enough to release the typescript and tear up the contract. That was on a Wednesday. On Thursday, David drove round with a second copy of the typescript to Malcolm Edwards at Gollancz. Malcolm read the whole thing over the weekend. On Monday we were in possession of a new improved Gollancz contract. And had the benefit of Malcolm's knowledgeable sub-editing.

After *Billion* came *Penguin Science Fiction Omnibus*, an amalgamation of the three individual Penguin anthologies. It was published in 1973, and has never been out of print since, despite all the changes at Penguin.

No doubt I should then have been getting on with my Stubbs saga, but writing *Billion* had renewed a taste for *Frankenstein*, together with an absorption in the life of Mary Shelley and those of her circle. Mary Shelley's intense and ultimately enigmatic novel reflects much of the traumas of her childhood and of her life with the poet Shelley. Even the monster's proposed immolation seems to be an oneiric reference to Shelley's funeral pyre. Mary Shelley makes us aware of mysterious congruences between life and fiction.

Nor is *Frankenstein* solely a reflection of her life and Shelley's. It owes a great deal to her father, William Godwin, and his *Caleb Williams*, or *Things As They Are*, that great novel of vengeance and exposure of the injustices of society, themes which emerge strongly in his daughter's best novel.

Moved partly by exegetical impulse, and by the hope of extracting Mary's novel from the misrepresentations of the movies, I wrote *Frankenstein Unbound* (1973). But circumstance has doubled back on me, and my novel has now been filmed by Roger Corman in Italy, as *Roger Corman's Frankenstein Unbound*. That foundling of Mary Shelley's, the monster, has found many homes – and no resting place.

Also in the mid-seventies, I wrote a non-fiction book, *The Shape of Further Things*, which centres round Heath House, a pleasant Regency house in which Margaret and I and our growing family then lived. Sad to say, the house is now threatened with demolition, despite all we have done to try to save it. Once upon a time, it was marked and named on the Ordnance Survey 1-inch map of the area. But developers got it.

The same period saw the publication of *The Malacia Tapestry*, which was inspired by my interest in G. B. Tiepolo – not merely his paintings, but the curious "Capricci" and "Scherzi" he engraved towards the end of his life. That novel was published by the redoubtable Tom Maschler at Jonathan Cape, who put his hand on the manuscript and said, with his usual enthusiasm, "I will not change a word of it."

My heart sank. I thought it needed copy-editing.

Tom published *Malacia Tapestry* with Tiepolo engravings as illustrations – the first Cape novel to carry illustrations, according to Tom.

Both Cape and Harper & Row in the States used the same jacket for their hardcover editions, wrap-arounds of cool Tiepolo *Scherzi*, "Magicians with four figures near a smoking altar", and "Half-dressed nymph with two children, surrounded by four men". That raffish world of Tiepolo's, seedy yet glamorous, cluttered with emblems of an unknown past, skulls, bronze altars, urns with ram's heads, swords, shattered pines, and the tomb of Punchinello, possessed my imagination for many hours and many days.

With the paperback editions, problems arose.

Malacia sold in the States to a paperback house, Ace books, for the same price I had been getting fifteen years earlier. Ace marketed it with a jacket showing people in funny medieval costume and a dinosaur ripping the bodice off a well-favoured young female person.

The edition sold well. Susan Alison, my editor at Ace, wrote to tell me they were going to reprint. I wrote saying that now maybe we could have a better jacket. Susan wrote back saying that it was the jacket which sold the book. I'm sure she was right.

Granada, with British paperback rights, created a Victorian jacket. It was totally unacceptable. I saw it by accident while in their offices. An argument developed. Granada could not use a black and white jacket like Cape's; it would look as if not enough money had been spent.

"Then use the 'Scherzi' and I'll colour them for you myself."

165

The offer was not accepted. I was told that if I continued to be difficult, a plain typographical jacket would be used.

"Great," I said.

Eventually, Nick Austin, my staunch editor friend, rescued the situation. The published jacket shows merely a mythological beast, not unlike the old Supercortemaggiore animal seen on Italian filling station signs, together with a dubious compliment from Eric Korn in the *TLS*: "The best novel Brian Aldiss has written for a long time."

Karel Thole painted a sumptuous cover for the German Heyne edition of *Malacia*. But my city state owed more to Ragusa and beleaguered Istra than to a pampered Venice or Urbino.

Tom Maschler was a good inventive publisher. In that he resembled Tony Godwin, as well as in his energy and sense of not exactly belonging to the English system – a feeling I shared. When I remarked casually that he had never put out a selection of my short stories, he said at once, "Send me some – I'll publish them."

The result was *Last Orders*, which in its nervous intensity, awareness of future arts and sciences, its anguish and humour, remains the volume that sums up my difficult 1970s. The casual yet attentive way Tom Maschler published it was admirable.

I submitted *Last Orders* to an American publisher. The collection was a bit extreme for him. "Why don't you throw out a couple of these 'Enigma' things and put in some stories about space travel, of the kind you do so well? Otherwise I can't publish it."

"Well, no, look – I mean, this is *Last Orders*, and this is the way it is. The stories are the way I want them. Dilution would spoil it."

"Brian, they're only stories."

"Not to me."

So the book didn't get publication in the States. That is, not until the successes of *Helliconia* and *Forgotten Life*, when Kent

Carroll of Carroll & Graf published an immaculate edition – twelve years after Cape, but not a word changed.

Brothers of the Head followed *Last Orders*. It was published by the short-lived (but exciting) Pierrot Press, with illustrations by Ian Pollock, then an unknown name. Like Mary Shelley's *Frankenstein, Brothers* is based on a dream. I was driving back from Old Hunstanton with Margaret and Wendy in the Volvo. I said, "I've just remembered – I had an awful nightmare. Too terrible to tell you."

"Oh, go on," they said. "Tell us."

So I did.

One day, someone will film *Brothers of the Head*. Already, several options have ticked by.

Weidenfeld came to life again. Two editors took me to lunch in 1977 and asked when I was going to deliver the next Horatio Stubbs novel. They said something which to this day I find hard to credit.

They told me that they had received more correspondence over *The Hand-Reared Boy* and *A Soldier Erect* than any other novels ever published by the company.

"We had three sacks full. It was amazing."

"Where are these sacks?"

"We burnt them. We didn't want you to be bothered with them."

Those were my letters and I should have had them.

Despite this revelation, I went ahead and wrote what was to prove the end of the Stubbs saga, *A Rude Awakening*, set in Medan, the capital city of Sumatra. It was intended in part as a valedictory to the Fourteenth Army, then breaking up – that "Forgotten Army" of General Slim's, forever embedded in the hearts of all who served in its ramshackle ranks. It is also a novel about love and betrayal, and is the only novel about that particular British campaign, obscure, disastrous and illuminating as it was. Finally it was the novel I had first attempted to write while back in England on demob leave. It was to have been my bulletin to the English people.

But somehow thirty years had passed. *A Rude Awakening* did not achieve half the attention of its predecessors. Perhaps the bulletin was a bit late . . .

Medan, Malacia, Ermalpa, Avernus

As I was writing about Medan, that city which had so enchanted me, I realised I had already translated it on to paper. My city of Malacia, suspended under a curse of non-change, had been shaped by my experience of the Sumatran capital. Now, as I dwelt again in imagination among its stained walls and broken roofs, I saw that by writing the fantasy I had freed myself – after thirty years – to write about the real thing.

Only it had ceased to be the real thing. Medan had utterly changed. It had been overtaken by the internal combustion engine and the population explosion. To my eyes, it was a far less appealing place in 1979 than it had been in 1945.

It had never seemed possible that I could get back to that tropical island. I was aware of Proust's melancholy words of wisdom, that we can never return to a place we loved, because we are looking for a past time as well as a place. Nevertheless, when the opportunity arose to visit Sumatra, I seized it.

An Australian fan phoned me at home and invited me to be Guest of Honour at a convention in Melbourne.

"Thanks. Can I have forty-eight hours to think it over? I'll phone you back, saying definitely one way or the other."

In fact, I phoned him back the next day, saying I was keen to accept the invitation.

"Oh dear. We've invited Roger Zelazny instead. We thought you'd say no."

They fixed things up, in the resourceful manner of fans everywhere, and I flew out to Australia.

On the way, I stopped in Singapore. From there, it was easy to take a package tour to Sumatra, to Medan . . .

Thirty-three years since I had left. I was still in pretty good nick; Medan had changed more than I. Shadows and silences had been banished, along with the bullock carts. The city streets echoed to the sound of pip-squeak hooting. Mopeds and three-wheelers were everywhere. Children swarmed amid the traffic. The air, thick and heavy, was poisoned by exhaust gases. The Third World – a term uncoined in my day – reeled under its own prodigality.

Much else was altered, including the political system. Since the revolution, the colonial Dutch masters had been evicted; Sumatra was part of the Muslim Republic of Indonesia. Streets and buildings had been renamed. Roads had multiplied. Peaceful kampongs had disappeared under concrete. Now, complex one-way systems were choked with traffic.

During my year in Medan, I had lived in a colonial-style house which had served as a brothel during the Japanese occupation. I was happy there. According to scientific reports, extra sunlight improves health and morale; more energy flows to the system. It is exhilarating to see the sun go fizzing up to zenith every day of the year in Sumatra. The best it can manage on the latitude of London is to climb to 62 degrees above the horizon on the longest day. Just to sit and read is a habit of cooler climes.

Braving Medan's traffic, I left the Danautoba Hotel with an English-speaking guide called Michael, determined to discover my old home and, if possible, set foot in it once again.

We caught a taxi. Then began a tour of the town. Places I recognised faded into unknown mazes of streets. Could it be that what I had known as the Kesawan was now the roaring Jalan Singamangaraja? Well, "Be sure you are in good hand

170

of us," as the local guide put it, and Michael was encouraging. We drove on, and around, and around.

We did eventually arrive in an area I thought I recognised, although we had approached it from a direction which would have been impossible in the forties.

"It must be near here," I said hopefully. Thirty-three years – memories, however vivid, are no more to be relied on than guidebooks.

Trees had come down and fences had gone up. Michael and the taxi man both started worrying on my account. On one corner, I saw a house standing back from the road which could have been mine. When I got out and looked at it, Michael went over and knocked at the door. Some Indonesians emerged; they chanced to belong to Michael's tribe, so everyone was friendly, and I was ushered in. Chances were that it was my old billet, but I saw now that this wasn't going to be so easy.

The parents and their brothers and sisters were under thirty years old; between them they had a clutch of children who stood, smiling and courteous, sometimes on one leg, as I sat down in their kitchen and drank coffee with them. They knew nothing of Dutch rule, never mind British or Japanese. History is diffuse when Malay verbs can be of any tense. Had this been my house? they asked.

Well, had it? Memory was as nebulous as history.

I wasn't sure. It certainly looked like my house, but I used to enter through a door on the other side. I had lived upstairs.

Would I like to look upstairs? They could easily get Grandad out of bed.

Oh, I don't want to trouble Grandad . . .

As we proceeded upstairs, kids and all, I thought, No, you're mad, Aldiss – the staircase went the other way round, or else you actually have forgotten.

"That was my room," I said, pointing to a closed door on the landing. Best put a bold face on it. Too late to call it off now. Pretend you're not eccentric.

171

They opened up. Grandad and I exchanged greetings, and I walked round the room. A curious creepy feeling stole over me, compounded of amazement, delight, and the dregs of time. Yes, by a miracle it was my room, still in the world of things that were. I gazed from the window; the view was broadly the same, the same lovely tropical trees, though more houses crowded in. I turned to my hosts, beaming, thanking them all, saying how pleased I felt to come back.

But. As we were leaving the room, I thought, Hey, there used to be a balcony. There's no balcony. This can't be your room . . .

Still, the tropics are the tropics. Balconies fall off sometimes.

We went outside, Michael photographed us all, and we took the glad news back to the waiting taxi. Fond waves all round . . .

To this day, I don't know whether I got back to my old house or not. Some days I think I did, some days I think I didn't. I'm content with that uncertainty. Uncertainty is enriching, the very stuff of which life is made. We cannot wish ever to reduce life to a diagram. It was J. M. W. Turner with his apparent lack of form who understood Reality, not his rivals, secure in the Academy, plastering on their regulation bitumen. It was never possible for me to be sure one way or the other whether I had revisited my old house. That's the way it is: final but ambiguous; ambiguous but final.

That trip back in time brought forth a slender book. *Foreign Bodies* is my book of stories about the East. Much of it was written in Singapore or on a Boeing belonging to that kindest of airlines, Singapore Airlines. In Singapore I stayed with Sandie and Kirpal Singh and Rosie Ong and Tan Teck Meng. With the latter couple, I visited Sumatra. On that excursion I wrote one of my short stories on which I set some store, "A Romance of the Equator". It appeared first in *Foreign Bodies*.

Foreign Bodies, for which I designed the cover, was published in Singapore in 1981, and is dedicated to my friends there. It has never been reprinted elsewhere; I was too pleased to have had a book published in – to give it the ghostly title which is current – the Third World.

It remains a souvenir of that trip, a trip I suppose I do not have to make again.

After my journey to the East, I became ambitious to write novels which would encompass more generously my knowledge of the world in which I lived. It happened that on the last day of a visit to Sicily I stood on a quayside looking north over the Mediterranean. Suddenly, there came into my head, whole and clear, an entire novel.

Such abundance occurs fairly regularly with short stories. It had happened previously with novels; but I have never written them down, too busy with other things. This one I resolved to impale on paper at once.

I flew home to find my mother dying. At that time I was Chairman of the Society of Authors' management committee, and had to go up to London to attend the AGM. There were other harassments. I shall always be grateful to my wife for saying, in her uninsistent way, as I was leaving our house, "You'd better go and see your mother first." I took a rosebud from the garden, peeled off its thorns and pressed it into my mother's hand where she lay. She knew me. Unable to open her eyes, she murmured, "How was Sicily?"

That afternoon, just before I mounted the platform to read out to the Society a summary of the year's activities, a member of staff came up and told me that my mother had died.

It was my mother who encouraged me to make little books and tell stories when I was still small enough to sit on her lap. She nourished my ambition to write.

So I wrote the novel I had in mind, which is entitled *Life in the West*, including in it my mother's death. It is set in the fictitious city of Ermalpa, on the real island of Sicily.

The last piece of dialogue in the book is, "How was

Ermalpa?"

Life in the West was published on 6 March 1980. That generous man, Anthony Burgess, included it in his *Ninety-Nine Best Novels*. The American edition – slightly delayed – is published in 1990, by Carroll & Graf.

The faults as well as the virtues of that novel were apparent to me. I decided to have another attempt at the same kind of subject. My wife presented me with a greetings card on which she had made additions to the printed words, so that it reads, "To Wish You Success with Life in the West, and the Best of Luck with Helliconia".

The magical power of a word. It was in the summer of 1977 that I had written a letter to a friend, Philip Dunn, setting forth in outline how I imagined existence would be for a human-like race living on a planet resembling Earth whose year was several thousands of ordinary years long. Philip and his wife Jane were Pierrot Books. "Let's say this planet is called *Helliconia*," I said, on inspiration. The word was out. From then on, Helliconia increasingly filled my thoughts. Of course, what eventually emerged was unlike *Life in the West*.

In order to display the long seasons of Helliconia to their best effect, it was necessary to spill over from one volume to three. Four might have appeared more logical, one for each of the four seasons; but one must not tax a reader's patience too greatly. I'm no Vivaldi.

Two years were spent on research into all the background knowledge required. Living in Oxford has its compensations: there are many learned men one can talk to. I was encouraged by J. M. Roberts's daring one-volume history of the world, which appeared in hardcover as *The Hutchinson History of the World* (this title had to be changed when the work appeared from Penguin Books). It was typical of the imaginative quality of John Roberts's mind that he includes as the last illustration in his book an Alex Schomburg cover painted for *Fantastic*, issue of October 1961. (I had reproduced it myself in my large format volume *SF Art*.)

It was Roberts who gave me, over lunch, a good idea of how civilisation would continue, in codified and probably militaristic form, even during the centuries of Helliconian winter. He was beginning to plan his BBC television series, *The Triumph of the West*, which has very much the sort of narrative line I aimed for in *Helliconia*.

How is it, Roberts asks, that explorers from the West voyaged all over the globe in perilously small boats? Never a Chinese junk or dhow from the world of Islam docked at Southampton.

The answer must lie in not only the inventiveness but the curiosity behind that inventiveness which is a characteristic of Western man. It is the impulse which permits us to view Neptune and its moon system through the eyes of a Voyager. Again, that kind of curiosity – that putting together of two and an unknown two – was to be celebrated in *Helliconia*.

Finally I arrived at the point where I could begin writing; the three volumes were completed in only five years, making seven years gestation all told.

Helliconia became actual, its citizens dear to me; but of course all authors say that. A place I liked and believed in was Oldorando – even more ramshackle than Medan had been in AD 1945. Although I was ill and under pressure, the writing of those novels meant a deep and satisfying extension of experience.

In particular, I liked my lovely Queen Myrdemingala in the middle volume. I worried for her, and was sorry when the years carried her away. But writers can't help that sort of thing: they merely depict toned-down versions of what happens in "real life".

Readers wonder how writers create characters; writers wonder how to explain. They arise in context. I am conscious of what Samuel Johnson says in his *Life of Pope*, that "the greater part of mankind *have no character at all*, have little that distinguishes them from others equally good or bad"; and he goes on to talk of how easy it is to utter the same praises over

175

different tombs.

Sometimes a gesture or a word starts a character to life in the mind. Jim Lovelock's Gaia hypothesis proposes that all life in Earth's biosphere is an organism formed by a single evolutionary process; that a multifarious organism unconsciously regulates the factors which make life on the planet comfortable, and has done so for billions of years, despite (for instance) the Sun becoming about 25 per cent hotter during that period.

I wanted to incorporate this revelatory view of the unity of life on more than one level. So the human hunters in the first Helliconia volume are shown as creatures of their climate as much as the animals they hunt. I have one of my strong men, Aoz Roon, scoop water up from a river with his hand to drink. Some of the water falls away, back to the river. The droplets strike the gleaming water. And that insignificant gesture is witnessed a thousand light years away, a thousand years later, on Earth. There are many such linkages in the novels. I envied the multitudinous peoples of my planet, for all the hardships they undergo. Life's no harder on Helliconia than it is on Earth: we don't all live in Santa Barbara, Surrey or the Côte d'Azur.

The stars in the case of our earthly drama are human men and women – at least according to human men and women. No doubt elephants, dolphins and cats think differently. But the fact of the matter is that all visible life forms could disappear from the stage and the show would still go on. Invisible life, microbes, bacteria, etc., far outweigh the visible. The importance of mankind lies mainly in its own eyes, for all that anthropic cosmology argues to the contrary.

Such is part of the none-too-palatable message of the Helliconia novels. What jacket should enfold the first volume? Selection of jacket is the author's chance to choose an illustration, a picture that will convey his theme to readers.

Of course, *Helliconia* is also a story of light, the glorious light without which we are nothing.

If light is your preoccupation, it is better to be a painter than a writer. Paint imitates light. Words imitate thought. Even Virginia Woolf in her most impressionistic prose cannot get the feel of the day as does Monet, Manet or Renoir. "The sun is God," said Turner, on his deathbed.

Altdorfer's great painting, *The Battle of Alexander*, or *Battle of Isus*, is an industrious painting, full of warring armies, sieges, alarums and excursions, like a great epic poem. Despite which, it manages to be also a study of light. The sky dwarfs all human activity.

A detail from the upper regions of this canvas provided the jacket for *Helliconia Spring*. One's hope is that Altdorfer would not be too vexed.

While I was writing the Helliconia novels, our accountant allowed us to fall into grave tax problems – problems embarrassingly well publicised. We sold up our lovely house and swimming pool and went to live in a semi-detached in North Oxford. My science fiction library was purchased by Dallas Public Library, where the Aldiss Archive is preserved in better condition than I could manage.

"Don't worry," I said to my wife. "It's not as if we've broken a leg. It's only money." But I took the precaution of sacking our accountant.

In the very week when I sent the typescript of *Helliconia Winter* to Jonathan Cape and Atheneum, I determined on a change of scenery. That day, we heard that the house where we now live was for sale. Next morning, a Saturday, my wife and I drove with the children to look it over.

Tim and Charlotte jumped out of the car shouting, "Buy it, buy it."

That afternoon I went round to see an architect friend. We sat under his apple tree and drank a bottle of white wine, after which I drove him up to look at the house. After a preliminary canter round, he was repeating what the kids had said.

I said to the owner, "I'll pay your asking price without haggling if you will say yes straight away."

177

"Yes," he said, "and we'll have a whisky on the deal."

A couple of hours later, I went back to Margaret and said, "I've jush bought a housh."

We moved in in time to hold my daughter Wendy's wedding reception here two weeks later.

But this is supposed to be a book about writing, not real life, hard though it is to separate the two, the twain.

After the long haul of *Helliconia*, we took a holiday in Greece, where my elder son Clive was working (the Helliconia novels are dedicated to him). There we climbed the slopes of sprawling Mount Helicon, the home of the Muses, and Margaret collected some plants from it.

Returning to England, I decided to work with David on *Trillion*, already mentioned. I could not have asked for a better friend and collaborator. My idea was that a non-fiction book would be a sort of convalescence. It was not so. Any more than this volume, which has taken four years of intermittent work, has been easy. In a novel, you always know what to leave out.

Further, fiction represents a special kind of articulateness. An American colleague, Rosemary Herbert, whose main study is English writers, is putting together a book of my conversations. For an academic press – American, of course. She has faith. My belief is that such ability as I have on paper springs from a kind of central inarticulacy. William Hazlitt speaks of the way in which a man "may feel the whole weight of a question, nothing relating to it may be lost upon him, and yet he may be able to give no account of the manner in which it affects him, or to drag his reasons from their silent lurking-places." That's good. That's it exactly.

And that is why this book is filled with small activities, whereas the central business of a writer's life is sitting still or walking about alone, lost in a brown study, waiting for something to emerge from its lurking-place. This is the raid on the inarticulate.

Something in our new family surroundings proved magical. Another personality was shed, a new one blossomed.

Whatever *Helliconia* did to its readers, it altered the mind of its author. Perhaps this should be one of the objectives of novels. I made life on Helliconia as challenging as I found life on Earth. The process softened me — and softened me towards myself, so that I could accept others more readily. I even found myself able to forgive my dead parents, as I hope my children will one day come to forgive me.

One tangible result of this new-found light was the novel *Forgotten Life*. Only a few other matters remain to be accounted for.

While writing *Helliconia*, while the volumes were appearing, I saw that a year was approaching — 1984 — in which I would have no book published, in the gap between *Summer* and *Winter*. Since this would break a thirty-year record, I became superstitious about it. Putting together a collection of non-SF short stories by which I set some store, I sent them to Cape.

We all knew that *Seasons in Flight* (a title making covert reference to the Helliconia books) would not sell many copies. But the people at Cape took as much care with it as they had with the novels. Again I was encouraged to choose the jacket. The choice was plain, a Czech picture which inspired the story called "The Blue Background". It came from a book published in Bratislava, sent me by Josef Nesvadba, our friend in Prague.

Reviewers had their usual pathetic problems with *Seasons in Flight*. What was Aldiss writing now? Was this SF or was it not? "The perceptive reader will find much to ponder" — *Hartford, Connecticut Courant*. "Ideal bedtime dip-in-book" — *Northamptonshire Evening Telegraph*. Makes your heart sink, doesn't it? The SF reviewers in the main simply treated the collection as SF.

Again I was accused of being gloomy. Surely, *surely*, some of those stories were comedy? Filled with excitement about the wild places of the world, and what William Godwin called the

179

wilderness of human society. At the height of his popularity, Charles Dickens was walking in the street with John Forster, complaining of his reception. Forster protested that he was more admired even than Thackeray. Dickens: "But I'm not appreciated *enough.*"

Every writer knows how Dickens feels.

Only difference is – Dickens was right.

My days at Cape were nearing an end. Tom Maschler came down to Oxford to persuade me to stay with the firm. We dined together in a little restaurant in North Parade, which had a good wine list. Tom lost the argument, I paid the bill.

Cape was in trouble and soon to be bought up. While *Helliconia* was current, I was often in their Bedford Square offices, and with members of their staff in taverns nearby. When it was finished, I walked into Publicity one day and was mistaken by a woman there for Bernard Levin, who had written a dotty if favourable review of *Life in the West*. The woman insisted I was Levin, despite my denials.

Gollancz became my new publisher. Malcolm Edwards was accustomed to the fact that I cannot write to order. I had also acquired a hardcover publisher in New York to publish my books irrespective of whether or not they were SF. Atheneum brought out, among other titles, *Helliconia, Trillion Year Spree, Seasons in Flight* and *Forgotten Life*. As mentioned, Carroll & Graf have also picked up some mislaid items, for which I am grateful.

But takeovers, the curse of present-day publishing, forced a change on both sides of the Atlantic. Is Hodder & Stoughton safe?

Authors do not necessarily have close contact with their paperback companies. Whereas one deals directly, or through the intermediary of an agent, with the hardcover publisher, a deal with the paperback company can be done mainly between hardcover and paperback firms (one often owns the other), again with only agent as intermediary. I had been published for many years before entering a paperback office.

Dot Houghton at New English Library invited me to their place in Barnard's Inn, London — friendly and Dickensian to a degree.

New American Library were also hospitable. They had just moved into the new J. C. Penney building in New York when my wife and I visited them. The open-plan arrangement, the nylon carpeting, the pictures on the walls, the flowers on the windowsills – all were new. Margaret went over to admire the plants.

"Don't touch the geraniums!" someone screamed. Too late. Static electricity sizzled between dainty fingers and leaves.

As a writer becomes established, he finds friends in the paperback houses. Warner Books publish the film tie-in edition of *Frankenstein Unbound*. I've known Brian Thomsen there for some years, and Nansey Neiman even longer, since she worked in England at Weidenfeld. Similarly, at the comparatively new company of Mandarin, in London, I have friends; they publish *Forgotten Life* in paperback, and have taken great care with resetting type to fit their format, and with the cover and blurbs. Blurbs: the cry of the vendor, the old cry "Buy me!" expanded to fifty deathless words.

Blurbs are sometimes unwittingly funny. I knew no one in Leisure Books in New York in 1975, when they stuck a blurb on one of my novels which read, "You may have to wait until 2001 to read a better Aldiss. But don't count on it."

Authors are not powerless in such matters. Patience and good humour are needed to outsmart the *fait accompli* – or, as I saw it written recently, the *fate accompli*. One has to remember that editors may be under worse pressures than authors. If an author feels himself under too much pressure, he has only himself to blame. Nor is there any use blaming one's agent. However it may appear at times, interests of agents and clients are not identical; if one relies too innocently on that strange friend-business relationship, one may be in for a rude awakening, to coin a phrase.

The going with A. P. Watt remained smooth until about

1985. I remained with Watt but was forced to look elsewhere for a media agent.

Frank Hatherley was the man I had the luck to find. Frank and I had worked together when he was story editor at the BBC. In the late seventies, BBC TV broadcast a series of Saturday night plays called *The Eleventh Hour*. The trick about them was this: each play had to be put together entirely within the week. Writers, producers, directors, technicians and casting manager all met together in Lime Grove on a Monday morning. The whistle blew. From then on, a storyline had to be agreed, the play written, the sets prepared, the actors chosen and rehearsed, and so on. A great deal of adrenalin flowed. The show went out live on the Saturday evening.

Two writers worked together each week. While Robin Chapman and I were still writing "Hot Local and Galactic News" on the Wednesday, the chief actor, Patrick Stewart, was rehearsing at our elbows. And Frank was our editor.

Now Frank and I got together and founded Avernus Creative Media. So far, Avernus (named after the observation station in *Helliconia*) has earned us little money, yet in many ways it is our pet, our pleasure.

Several TV schemes were floated under Frank's aegis. His most inspired idea so far is our roadshow. He put together an evening's presentation of sketches, playlets, and pieces selected from my prose and poetry. Now *Science Fiction Blues* has played one-night stands all over England. We toured it, and still give performances as and when the opportunity arises. We took it to Munich.

Three actors do the show. With me are Ken Campbell and Petronilla Whitfield, who are brilliant. Both Ken and the glamorous and amusing Petronilla have extensive stage experience, and Frank is our stage manager. We work well together.

Avernus has published the book of *Science Fiction Blues*, with illustrations. Our first publication. Other books to come. This development is as pleasing as it is unexpected, a diversion in a writing life. It is easy to understand how Charles Dickens became a slave to his public readings.

Every writer with any originality has to attempt to create a climate of opinion whereby his voice can be appreciated, whether by a large audience or small. My hope with *SF Blues* is that, by speaking direct to the people out front, that kind of contact is made. On nights when the show is on, Ken Campbell and I visit the bar beforehand and afterwards, to talk to members of the audience who are interested. Ken, of course, is a genius. If he were in America instead of England, he would be world-famous, instead of just a legend in his own lifetime.

Our latest performance of *SF Blues*, under the less committed title of *Last Orders*, was held at the country home of our friends, Alex and Felicity Duncan, before an invited audience of seventy – to be followed by an al fresco meal.

As Petronilla, Ken and I were taking our bows at the end, someone called from the audience, "Brian, you should give up writing and become an actor!"

"That's what my publisher tells me," I replied.

Neither TV series or *SF Blues*, however much excitement they bring, is as important as a novel into which so much experience is poured. However, "it will not always happen that the success of a poet is proportionate to his labour," as Johnson reminds us. All writers secretly know this, and tremble.

CHAPTER 17

From Oxford to Italy

One of the great pieces of fortune which has attended my generation is the way in which the world has opened up. It has been possible to broaden one's horizons.

This year, 1989, I have been twice to Italy and twice to Canada, led there by the reception my novels have enjoyed. Of course, that reception is modest compared with some others; for instance, Salman Rushdie's *The Satanic Verses* was published in England within a few days of *Forgotten Life*. Rushdie's novel became almost immediately one of the most famous novels of its time.

Forgotten Life concerns the question of fantasy, how much of our lives is fantasy, and how fantasy can provide either an escape clause or a trap. All three main characters, as they move through the predicament of life in comfortable Oxford circles, use fantasy, constructively or destructively.

The novel was published in the United States and in Canada shortly after the British edition, each using the striking Lucian Freud painting as cover art.

The visit to the launch in Toronto, where my publishers were hospitable, was more than educational. The reviewer in the *Toronto Globe*, Elspeth Cameron, gave me my longest and most thoughtful review.

Although the English reviewers mainly admired *Forgotten*

Life, the warmest praise came as usual from American reviewers. The *New York Times,* the *Washington Post,* the *LA Times,* were all friendly. Especially pleasing was Samuel Hynes in the *New York Times,* who even got in a good word for my imaginary poet, William Westlake, some of whose verse appears in the book. Hynes says of this verse that it "makes me wish he had existed and had finished the poem".

Publication day is a time of anxiety. That proud hunter, the writer, becomes the hunted. Now, if ever, one is maligned and misunderstood. Self-regard is at stake. All the relish the writing of the novel engendered disappears. What is left is the casual judgment of reviewers, who often have read none of one's previous work. I should know. I was a regular reviewer for about twenty years.

Occasionally – the miracle. A reviewer who has read all one's books!

Forgotten Life won a very favourable review from Australia, from Bruce Gillespie, writing in the Melbourne *Age.* Bruce stands as an exemplar of a science fiction aficionado. Ever since 1969, he has poured his lifeblood into his amateur magazine, *SF Commentary* – amateur in the best sense, for it printed perceptive criticism of science fiction novels, stories, and trends, such as one rarely finds elsewhere. For a while, Bruce liked nothing he read, and denounced the whole mode. He disliked my Helliconia novels, and said so.

As well as criticism, *SF Commentary* carries the story of all Bruce's personal troubles. Along with the latest adulation of Stanislav Lem went the story of Bruce's failures with girls or – a recent event – the death of his father. Bruce visited England once, and stayed with Chris Priest, who was disturbed to find that his Australian guest ate poached eggs with his fingers. We three drove down to Stonehenge one sunny day, before Stonehenge was railed off from the public.

In 1969, when *SF Commentary* began, Mike Moorcock's *New Worlds* was still thriving, and Gillespie and his merry men, John Foyster and the others, set upon it eagerly and

185

understood it (even when they did not like its contents) in a way given to no other group of readers. Their comments remain fresh. I was praised for some of the original *Barefoot in the Head* stories in Issue 1 and damned for another in Issue 2. I also, I'm proud to say, had an article in Issue 2. Of course, no one got paid for their work. We never expected it in the SF field of yore. I have written thousands of words on such terms, for many fanzines which have proved far more ephemeral than Gillespie's publication.

Perhaps one day some omniscient omnivore will examine the relationship between published and privately printed activity in the SF field, and show the literature for what it is – a tremendous populist movement of the century. He will surely have to reckon with the prickly intellects of Bruce Gillespie's *SF Commentary*.

Clarissa Rushdie at my literary agency sent me the text of what Anthony Burgess said about my novel. "Brian Aldiss has again turned from science fiction to the regular novel, with triumphant success. This is a subtle, moving and highly original examination of human relations in present-day England which made me forget a day's meals and excited me more than anything else I've read this year."

What word do I like best in this marvellous message? "Again."

Gollancz were careful to distance *Forgotten Life* from my science fiction. Someone, perhaps the retailer, lacks courage when it comes to authors whose writing falls into different modes.

Forgotten Life was my first book to have a Canadian publisher. The Canadian publishing industry is flourishing, but – like Australia – has a struggle disentangling itself from the rival American and British markets. Canadian rights were traditionally taken either by American or British publishers.

My agents cut the knot, reserving my Canadian rights and auctioning the book in Canada. Eight publishers were involved in the auction. Seven swore they liked the novel greatly but thought that since my name was too well known as an SF writer, a "straight" novel would be difficult to promote. Only Doubleday Canada had the courage to buy it.

This news was phoned to me by Clarissa. We discussed it, I professed myself satisfied and she rang off. After an hour, she rang back.

"Brian, you sounded so disappointed with the Canadian offer. If you don't think the money's sufficient, I could ring Gollancz and see if they would buy Canadian rights for a little more."

It was good of her to be concerned. But I never worry over money. I told Clarissa that my voice, as ever, was too expressive; I'm no poker player. What hit me was the thought that, after thirty years of my campaigning, people still think in these rigidly confining categories. I had just been turned down by seven competing publishers because I wrote SF.

Clarissa understood.

Here is how the *Sunday Times* managed one of its book supplement pages. *Forgotten Life* and Emma Tennant's *A Wedding of Cousins* were reviewed together in a box at the bottom of the page, getting about equal space. *Life* was summed up as "a cleverly worked, humane and philosophical fiction", while Tennant also received good marks. Above us, the rest of the page was devoted to one book, which received slightly more column inches than Tennant and I did between us. This was Joan Collins's *Prime Time*. There was also an attractive photo of the lady.

Is it mean-minded to say that of course the *Sunday Times* was not going to like Miss Collins's novel? And they didn't. Even its dedication was mauled over. Emma Tennant and I are well-established writers; if our books were so good, they needed more space for discussion and, if Miss Collins's book was so bad, it needed less. But there was that striking photograph of her.

Chaucer's attitude to publication was an open one: "Go, litel booke, go litel myn tragedie . . . " The book must make its own way in the world, like a grown child. But it is not every parent who can wave farewell to even a grown child (or a grown child who wishes to be waved farewell).

As I have demonstrated, writers exhibit anxiety responses to the way in which proffered work is received. This can seem trivial and ridiculous, even to the sufferer as he suffers, and completely out of scale with the grand perspectives of the work involved; yet it relates closely to the personality of the author, who, as we saw in Chapter Four, may be of a characteristically depressive nature, using the term in its clinical sense. He may most readily assert himself through his writing and be, in real life, uneasy about an assertion of individuality; from which it follows that his most valid self-expression comes through his work rather than through himself. This is why admirers often find their favourite authors disappointing in the flesh. (And, of course, not authors alone; actors also, while painters tend to be more articulate on canvas than in person.)

For what follows, we cannot do better than quote again from Anthony Storr's *Dynamics of Creativity*. After saying that a depressive personality may hold the work, rather than the person, as a focus for self-esteem, he goes on:

Many people of this temperament, during the course of childhood and adolescence, give up hope of being loved for themselves, especially since they habitually conceal their real natures. But the hope raises itself again when they start to create; and so they become intensely sensitive about what they produce, more sensitive than they are about their own defended personalities in ordinary social life. To mind more about one's book or painting than one does about oneself will seem strange to those who are sure enough of themselves to *be* themselves in social relations. But if a book or a painting contains more of the real person than is ever shown in ordinary life, it is not surprising that the producer of it is hypersensitive. A good example is Virginia Woolf, who went through agonies every time she produced a new book, and was desperately vulnerable to what the critics said about it, in spite of the fact that most of them were her intellectual inferiors. Her depressive temperament manifested itself in recurrent attacks of depression and finally in her suicide.

Well, I don't quite fit into that category. I am more likely to jump into the next novel than into the Thames. But I do have mixed feelings about publication days.

Forgotten Life is a consistent development based on all I have previously written. I realise it even has something of the same ground plan as *Non-Stop*; the riddles of the present may be solved by a scrutiny of the past. As a general principle it is not a bad one. The content of *Forgotten Life* would have surprised me four years ago. That's good – more important than the damned reviews.

My wife says of a new collection of my stories that they all concern survival. That may be the case, though it never occurred to me. One thing they have been about is a retreat from a reverential position vis-à-vis the Deity. After my non-conformist upbringing, God has always been a bother.

It would have been good to be an untroubled atheist, like the late philosopher A. J. Ayer – with whom I once sang "Blues in the Night" in duet, incidentally. Only when I had worked through the three volumes of *Helliconia* was I finally free of God. My anima had a chance to breathe. God hates animae, they're so immoral.

The world is full of injustice. Despite which, a sense of justice glows within us, like an impossible dream of utopia. Injustice becomes institutionalised every time there is a war, as the present excited state of *glasnost* Europe reminds us; victorious and defeated nations alike impose repression on their populations. There are exceptions. Germany is a remarkable example of a nation which, after defeat, has developed a just life for its citizens, as these things go (I speak only of West Germany, of course).

The inhabitants of my spaceship in *Non-Stop* are victims of injustice of a public kind; the three main protagonists of *Forgotten Life* suffer from private injustices. Our political institutions permit only rough justice. If we admit it, we are ourselves often unjust. Can our flaws be redeemed – not by the irrational threats of punishment uttered by established religions, but by rational endeavour?

Deep-seated impulses within us move towards aggression on one hand and submission on the other. Both these impulses we hold in common with the mammals; and not the mammals only – with crayfish, even. Aggression and submission are our inheritance from a distant pre-human ancestry, and a part of the mechanism whereby life goes forward on this planet.

This is the law: that sometimes we are victorious, sometimes we must submit. Publication of a book is a faint, ironic echo of real battles for survival long ago, when defeat might entail exile from the group, or submission a chance to fight again. We live our intellectual lives as best we can, reluctantly made aware that there are departments of one's self which function autonomously, beyond control of our consciousness.

This is why most discussion of politics and questions of war and peace – of disarmament, for example – are beside the point. What reason decides is what unreason can overturn.

Submission – bowing and scraping – is as prevalent as waving guns and swords. Patriotism, a noisy art, manages to amalgamate both propensities; while swearing our lives to king, country or flag, we also threaten our enemies; fair-haired patriotism has a swarthy brother, racism. Given a million years, we may by training and understanding extirpate these archetypes from our systems. They were needed in the past. In the present, they form a dangerous component of our societies.

*   *   *

190

Our first journey to Italy this year comprised a stay in Urbino and a World SF meeting in San Marino.

When Harry Harrison made his first sale to the celebrated SF magazine *Astounding* (later *Analog*), he put the money into a one-way flight to England and came here with his wife and young son. Since then, he has lived in a dozen countries and become an international man. When he and Joan settled in Dublin in the mid-seventies, they discovered little science-fictional activity there, and immediately set about drumming some up. The result was that they held two professional conventions, one in Dublin and one in Dun Laoghaire. Participants came from all round the world at Harry's bidding, as they would have done for few other people. There we founded World SF – again at Harry's bidding.

A feature of WSF meetings is the report from national secretaries on SF activity in their countries. This generally includes accounts of how many titles are published in hardback and how many in paperback; and, more importantly, how many titles are written by native authors and how many are translations from foreign authors. American and British secretaries are seldom able to speak of translations into English.

Last year in Budapest, I delivered the British report since our secretary was indisposed. Rejecting the quantitative approach, I named Doris Lessing's *The Fifth Child* as the most important fantasy – if it was legitimate to apply that label – published during the preceding year.

After the session talking to Sakyo Komatsu, whom I first met in Tokyo in 1970, I complained about the meaninglessness of most statistics and the length of some of the reports. Komatsu proposed to the delegates that in future all speeches should last for only two and a half minutes and contain at least one joke.

Komatsu-san's novel *Japan Sinks* has probably sold more copies around the globe than any other novel which proclaims itself as SF (this excludes such novels as *1984* and *Brave New*

World). At Expo '70 he was one of the designers of Future World in Mitsubishi's technology tower. He is Chairman of the Japanese SF Writers. When he was dining with us one evening, in the famous baroque Restaurant Hungaria in Budapest, he told us that some of his members are extremely rich. They write complex computer games programmes, several of which can take up to a year for even an expert to unravel. They earned, he said, x billion yen every year. Harry asked him how much that was in American dollars.

"About four-five million American dollars," Komatsu said. There was a long reflective silence round the table.

The arrangements in Hungary were good. Presiding was Peter Kuczka, supported by Peter Szabo. Meetings were usually held in the publishing house, Mora Ferenc, a new office block in a suburban road in Budapest, the offices from which some of my stories have been published.

At one point, I sat outside the offices among trees – think of that, you Western publishers in London, New York, Munich – and was interviewed by two Bulgarians from Sofia Radio.

They asked, If I could change one factor in the world as it is at present, what would it be?

The question had political and technological overtones. I gave a psychological response.

My answer was that I would reorganise some of the pathways in the curious structure of the human brain. Owing to the particular evolutionary development of *Homo sapiens*, the brain contains three layers, the (outer) neocortex being the most recent. Connections between these layers are not of the best. For instance, it seems that in moments of extreme emotion – fear, anger, love – the neocortex cannot interpose itself between us and our actions; it is bypassed: we "act without thought". Archetypes take over. (This, incidentally, is an argument against imposition of the death penalty on grounds of its deterrent effect: the terrorist or murderer about his business does not think; threats and laws do not exist for him when he is seized by compulsions originating from urges deeper than the neocortex.)

This obscurity in our complex thought processes means we are often estranged from our deepest motivations and do not understand why we act as we do or why we cling to false beliefs. We are sometimes riddles to ourselves. (No android will ever be built which can pass as human – that's fantasy.) My character Joseph in *Forgotten Life* exemplifies this: he lives most of his life under a mistaken assumption he has, for reasons of temporary survival, imposed upon himself, until he is able to resolve the riddle.

The art of psychoanalysis has shown us some pathways through the maze of our thoughts. If Sofia Radio gave me the power, I would make those pathways permanent from birth. We would then be in touch with ourselves and would perhaps no longer need false religions, horoscopes, shrinks and – who knows – threats of nuclear war.

Of course, being in touch with ourselves implies facing all kinds of challenges. Although better understanding is a great blessing, there is truth in what Mary Wollstonecraft, mother of Mary Shelley, says in her *Letters written During a Short Residence in Sweden, Norway, and Denmark:* "What a long time it requires to know ourselves; and yet almost everyone has more of this knowledge than he is willing to own, even to himself." Wollstonecraft herself embodies many of the contradictions we find in ourselves. She appeared to long for peace, yet her life was active and stormy. In that same book, she says, "Whatever excites emotion has charms for me." The Romantic creed in a nutshell.

Back to Budapest. One of Peter Kuczka's best ideas was to gather the WSF delegates on a large boat on the Danube and give us a day's cruise to Sentendre (for lunch) and back. We were thus enclosed in a large comfortable space with a bar, and scenery flowing smoothly by.

Among the people we met during the cruise was a Czech writer, Peter Toke. I have Toke's novel on my desk as I write. It is entitled *Oriasvilag* and, from the cover, which depicts small naked people in a vast floral jungle, you might think it was a translation of *Hothouse*. Not so. This is Toke's first novel, *Giantworld*. He is an artist, and the book contains some of his illustrations.

Toke told me the kind of anecdote writers like to hear. When he was a schoolboy in Prague, he went into a bookshop where he saw a copy of my *Yet More Penguin Science Fiction*, published in April 1964, when I was away in Jugoslavia. Toke knew no word of English then, yet the cover attracted him – as well it might, since it reproduced part of a painting by Matta, "The Angry One".

Schoolboy Toke saved up and bought the book, feeling that it had something to say to him. With the aid of a dictionary, he began painstakingly to translate. On the Danube, he showed me his copy, with Czech words inscribed in minuscule writing under their English equivalents.

The first sentence of my introduction runs, "The images are what attract me in science fiction, more even than the surprises and the ideas and the crazy plots." This startled Toke: it expressed what he believed. It propelled him into painting and writing.

Who was more grateful – he to me or I to him? It's always a miracle when words do not fall upon stony ground.

Also on Kuczka's boat trip were writers from the German Democratic Republic. In the mythology of the West, it was the DDR which possessed the grimmest image. No one could run more counter to that type-casting than Angela and Karlheinz Steinmuller, a husband-wife team with science degrees who recently moved into SF. We hope to visit East Berlin shortly to see more of them, and of Olaf Spittel, who writes critically on German SF. Incidentally, the Steinmullers' recent novel, *Windschiefe Gerarden*, contains fourteen full-page illustrations which I would describe – intending a compliment – as uncommercial in nature, almost abstract. How pleasant if publishers in the West copied that idea.

The spirit of *glasnost* emanating from the Soviet Union made the Budapest meeting the most cosmopolitan since Dublin. For the first time, individual Russians arrived on the scene. When later publishing plans were announced by Eremi Parnov, he said that my Helliconia trilogy would be published shortly in Moscow. This may be my first official publication there, apart from scattered stories and appearances in *samizdat*.

(How is it I have had any success in writing? Because I never fail to write. It is now six of the evening, Saturday 17 September. Charlotte baked us tasty buns for our tea while Margaret and I worked in the garden; but now I am at my desk again. The ladies watch the Olympic Games from Seoul on television.)

Good company was to be had in Budapest. The most memorable meal was taken al fresco at Gundel's, on a sunny Sunday afternoon, when Margaret and I entertained Harry and Joan, Sam Lundwall, Norman Spinrad and Lee Wood. Only our friend, Josef Nesvadba, the Czech writer, was missing. Sam cheekily immortalised this occasion on the cover of his *Jules Verne Magasinet* (February 1989).

Much has changed in Hungary since then. And in the DDR and all of Eastern Europe.

From Budapest, Margaret and I took the Orient Express to Vienna, city of *sacher torte* and *accidie*, and feasted on the Bruegels in the Kunsthistorisches Museum. That room of Bruegels, which contains his "Hunters in the Snow" – one of the world's great paintings – is worth a trip to Vienna in its own right.

Then a smooth, well-appointed German train, on to Salzburg and Munich. We stayed in Munich a week, and entertained friends, including two of my German publishers, and were entertained by them. It was Wolfgang Jeschke of Wilhelm Heyne Verlag, himself a writer of considerable repute, who published *Helliconia* in German, using for the cover of the first volume the detail of Altdorfer's magnificent "Battle of Alexander" already referred to. Altdorfer's canvas hangs in the Alte Pinakothek, only a short distance from Wolfgang's office.

Charlotte Franke, the translator, invited us to spend the day with her in the village of Ambach, on the Starnbergersee, to the south of Munich. It is a pretty part of Bavaria, and Charlotte has the whole upper floor of an old farmhouse with sweeping eaves and wooden balconies which yield views of the lake. Here Charlotte works to maintain herself and her daughter. Eight hours' translation a day. I admire her: she never gives up. It is the lesson writers need to learn.

All our children go abroad. Some have worked abroad. It was an example we set them when we were young. I remember how my sister and I longed to escape from England when we were children. It is no illusion that people are freer now, at least in that respect.

It is not easy to write about writing or composition. For some it is a light and pleasurable activity, for others a nervous strain. This book has proved harder to write than many novels. For I cannot say how the spark that provokes writing occurs.

Here is an example of what I cannot say. As mentioned earlier, I sold a short story to a movie-maker, a man for whom my admiration is great or I would not have done such a thing. He has thought about making a film, a major movie, from that story for at least twelve years. At one time, I worked with him. Our efforts came to nothing. He has not given up.

Last week, because of something a friend said on the subject, I protested to my wife over lunch, "But you can't make a movie out of that story. It's just a vignette, poignant and complete in itself . . . "

As I spoke, I saw how you *could* do the movie.

Everything came clear.

Excusing myself, I left the lunch table and went into the study to write down my solution. It took about four hundred words.

I cannot say how the solution arrived then, or why it did not arrive before. Nor can I say, of course, if the solution will be acceptable to my friend the director.

What I do know is that that moment of revelation is the sort of thing one lives for. That it arrives undeniably, with all the impact of truth. And that it leads ... God knows where ...

... To more work of course ...

But I am already involved with film work.

Here is where the second visit to Italy comes in.

Early this year, we received a call from Hollywood. The Mount Company wanted an option on *Frankenstein Unbound*, my novel published by Jonathan Cape and Random House in 1973.

Frank Hatherley rang a friend of ours in Los Angeles, another director, who said in *Variety* recently that I was like Ray Bradbury "but tougher". He told us good things of the Mount Company. For once, the option went through, and before long Margaret and I were giving dinner here for Roger Corman and his producer, Kobi Jaeger. It was one of those pleasant occasions when we all enjoyed each other's company and the meal and the wine were beyond reproach.

Roger Corman's name is legendary. He had not directed a film for nineteen years; with the encouragement of Thom Mount, he was returning to directing with the film he most wanted to make, "Roger Corman's Frankenstein". But he could not get a script that suited him. It says much for my popularity in California that a copy of my novel was not to be found anywhere. Eventually the library service dug up one hiding out in Oregon.

It was what Roger wanted. The movie now became *Roger Corman's Frankenstein Unbound*, and in no time it was going into production. Roger has always been a fast mover. He started filming in May.

Directors never want authors on the set. Roger was different. He invited Margaret and me to watch the filming in

Italy, at the pretty town of Bellagio, on Lake Como. Frank went with us, and we took the family along, Wendy as Avernus photographer, also Tim and Charlotte. It was wonderful to have them all there.

The film should be out before this book.

And after the meal at our home, when Roger and I were sitting back and chatting, I said, "Our hero survives everything. How do you feel about a sequel in which he returns?"

"What would that be?"

"'Dracula Unbound'."

"I like it. What would that be about?"

I made something up. Roger and Kobi were interested.

And *Dracula Unbound* will be the next book to follow this one.

Truly, a writing life is exciting.

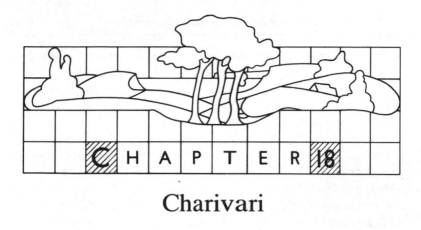

CHAPTER 18

Charivari

That old literary hero of mine, William Kinglake, who announced that his eyes were about to behold the splendour and the havoc of the East, reached Cairo and the Pyramids.

The Nile is still the artery of Egypt, as it was in ancient times, to which life and green things cling. All the rest is sand and desolation. The great river winds its way between desert and desert. In many places, the strip of cultivation following its course is less than a hundred metres wide. The symbolism for human lifespans is so intense that it is little wonder great and powerful religions grew up in the land of the Two Kingdoms.

At Aswan, you can inspect the High Dam, which controls the flooding of the great river and provides hydro-electricity for half the land. Behind it lies Lake Nasser, its waters still slowly expanding southwards. On the shores of this man-made lake lie the temples of Abu Simbel. These temples, some of the greatest surviving from the ancient world – and a monument to the egotism of Rameses II – were saved from the advance of the waters and raised piecemeal sixty-four metres above the flood by an act of international co-operation unprecedented in its scope.

Lake Nasser is visible from the gigantic doorstep of the temples. There is no dwelling, not so much as a hut, on its shores. Only the desert. And no sail on the waste of water. It now covers five hundred kilometres of what once was Nubia. To see it – to stare at it – is to long to heave oneself up on a camel and race southwards, southwards along that horrid shoreline to – God knows where.

Suppose one inspects the rescued temple, that mixture of modern and ancient miracles, before lunch. In the afternoon, if it is not too hot, one can – well, choices are many – one might sail in a felucca to the enchanted isle of Philae, where the goddess Isis may still be glimpsed, at least in imagination. Philae is her isle, dedicated to her.

But if by chance you are staying at the luxurious Oberoi Hotel on Elephantine Island, that chip in the Nile's flood, then you can walk through the hotel's gardens, and come upon a site that deserves commemoration in the intellectual history of the world.

Aswan is the ancient Syene, and it was here, almost on the Tropic of Cancer, that Eratosthenes noticed the sun shining down a deep well.

Eratosthenes was a great geographer, director of the famous library of Alexandria. His dates are variously given; one version I have is 276-194 BC. However that was, Eratosthenes was a sharp-eyed man. He observed that the sun shone vertically down the well at Elephantine, right to the bottom, at the time of the summer solstice. Whereas in Alexandria the sun's rays never fell perpendicular to the Earth's surface. In fact, a stake driven into the ground indicated by its shadow that the sun was seven degrees from zenith at summer solstice.

The distance between Syene and Alexandria was known. So Eratosthenes was able to calculate the circumference of the Earth from these figures.

Anyone with a little elementary mathematics could make the same calculation nowadays. What was so noteworthy in the case of Eratosthenes was his imagination. By looking down a hole in the ground he was able to deduce that the Earth was round – and to measure it. It was a wonderful perception. It meant that he was able to step outside his own *umwelt*, his perceptual universe, to perceive a new thing.

Aristarchus, as quoted by Archimedes, is another hero who managed as much. As far as we know, Aristarchus, whose name is memorialised on the Moon, was the first man on Earth to understand that the Earth revolved round the Sun and not vice versa. This scientific viewpoint enlarged our spiritual understandings. Such escapes from the small universes or *umwelts* into which upbringing seeks to bind us are always wonderful, and give hope for the human race.

What is appalling is that the truth did not prevail. Aristarchus was forgotten, his view derided – after all, one can *see* that the Sun goes round the Earth. And Aristotelian cosmology, which rejected heliocentricity in favour of the centrality of the Earth, prevailed over the next eighteen hundred years. Indeed, in a recent survey conducted in the United States, twenty-one per cent of the people questioned still believe that the Sun goes round the Earth. Is there hope for us? Are brains designed for fantasising rather than for logical thought?

How many centuries does it take for a fundamental truth to sink in?

Perhaps Jim Lovelock's Gaia hypothesis marks a similar perception to Eratosthenes' – a jump from a smaller to a larger *umwelt*. It promises truth – and not least because something akin to it was glimpsed long ago, in Lucretius' *De Rerum Natura*, which also shows delight regarding the complexity and interdependence of the world about us.

Although it is given to few of us to make wonderful discoveries, new perceptual breakthroughs are possible in the case of our own personalities. We too can look down the well inside us. My novel *Forgotten Life* celebrates this proposition.

It may be that we are stuck with a rigid view of our own personalities, that Aristotle has prevailed here also. Our personalities may be entirely more shifting than we give them credit for: that we speak, behave – and therefore think –

differently from one age to another, to a non-arbitrary extent not hitherto recognised. And these shifts may be a sign of strength, of the resilience of strength, which assist us as we grow from one age to the next, playing successive roles as baby, child, adolescent, youth, husband or wife, father or mother, grandfather or grandmother, widower or widow. For all these roles, we require new perceptions. Consistency is a dangerous virtue.

It is not easy to move to a new perceptual universe. For one thing it is uncomfortable. But someone once had to realise that the Sun was more than a light in the sky, that it was a physical object. In many lives, the revelation may be that – in the words of a cliché – we have only ourselves to blame. Or praise. There is no God dishing out rewards and punishments. As Shakespeare's Julius Caesar remarked, "The fault, dear Brutus, is not in our stars but in ourselves, that we are underlings." Or conformists. Or outlaws.

To enjoy Egypt, to appreciate its antiquity, one has to go underground, just as one has to travel into space to appreciate America's modernity. Europe – well, you just drive round it; it's there, voluptuous, extravagant, eroded, severe, civilised.

With the Soviet Union until recently one had to have almost a secret relationship. Of one's friends one was never too sure, though proofs emerged. For instance, when I was in Moscow in 1978, only one friend there dared to visit me in my hotel, or take me to his flat.

People came and went. Nothing was easy. We met in neutral capitals, where one smoked foreign cigarettes, drank well, ate badly, walked by unfamiliar rivers which flowed towards the sea through yet more hellish nations.

At one time, I knew somebody able to move easily between Moscow and London. Her name was Moura, Baroness Budberg, born Zakrevsky. She was famous in a mysterious way, for having been the lover of Maxim Gorky, H. G. Wells, and others. She was famous for a better reason: she was marvellous company.

Oddly enough, I knew of her long before meeting her, before I had heard of the Wells connection. Moura features in an exciting book – once quite celebrated – Robert Bruce Lockhart's *Memoirs of a British Agent*. When I first read that volume, how I envied Lockhart his excitements, in revolutionary Russia and elsewhere.

Moura was in her eighties when I met her, through another shadowy Russian friend. She then had an apartment in London's Cromwell Road, almost opposite what was the West London Air Terminal.

I used to visit her at six in the evening. Her flat was very dark and – so I thought – Slav, with heavy curtains, long mirrors, shiny floors and lots of books. Moura had a stout companion dressed in black who looked after her.

Moura would make an appearance, walking with a stick. Her limp got worse until the last time I saw her, when she said, airily, "I've had a plastic hip replacement. They threw the old bone to the doggies."

The phrase, with its reminder of Mr Mantalini's "demnition bow-wows", has always stuck in my mind.

The companion would be summoned. She would appear with a newly opened bottle of Smirnoff vodka and two small glasses on a silver tray. The bottle would be opened and poured. We would toast each other and drink. We conversed until we had finished the bottle between us; then I would make my farewells and leave.

Moura talked about Wells and other people she knew. I wish I had made a note of her conversation. Even at her advanced age, she had great charm. She was a woman who relished the company of men.

One day, she told me she could bear London no more. She wanted a warmer climate, and was going to live in Tuscany with one of her daughters. She went, and died within three months, an exotic woman in an exotic land.

Another daughter, Tania Alexander, whom Margaret and I

visited later in Oxfordshire, talked fondly of H. G. Wells. Her mother must have been a trial as a mother, and was missing for much of Tania's childhood in Estonia; but she speaks generously of her in her delightful book of reminiscence, *An Estonian Childhood*.

Moura Budberg was one of millions displaced by the Russian Revolution; she had to make her way through a world of lies and deceptions. As her daughter understands, she often made that way by using lies and deceptions herself.

To a greater or lesser degree, everyone's lives have been touched by the events of 1917, as Shelley's generation was touched by the French Revolution.

Before Gorbachev, when I heard people say they were going to Russia, I imagined it was like going into darkness: the darkness of the minds that governed the people.

The romance of nationalities. I've even written about a Belgian dentist. In *Helliconia Winter* I named my chief lady Lahl. Toress Lahl is captured in battle and enslaved. Having the feminist cause at heart, I studied books on slavery to get a taste of its misery. The name Lahl appealed since, in various spellings, it is common about the world. I knew a lady in Germany connected with publishing called Lahl, and once tried to sell my house to an Indian lady of the same name.

Narrative is what chiefly interests me in writing. I am a cause-and-effect addict.

Before beginning to write *Helliconia*, I had to brace myself to the task. I know a good many writers of an industrious persuasion who think nothing of producing a trilogy; to me it was more than an ordeal, it was a way of failing in literature. Before me lay the example, not only of countless stakhanovites in the SF and fantasy fields – of the sort later memorialised in the character of Sheila "Green Mouth" Winter in *Forgotten Life* – but of John Galsworthy, whose *Forsyte Saga* I loathe, which spun itself out into many volumes.

So I braced myself as William Godwin did when depressed, by reading Seneca. There's a particular power in reading the words of a long-dead author, even in translation. However, I did not get on with Seneca. I reread Lucretius' *De Rerum Natura* instead. I have known it since reading it in a Loeb volume in Parker's, long ago. It is a wonderful, speculative account of life on Earth, written in the first century BC, which effectively conjures up the mind of the man who dwelt upon those elemental matters. Lucretius can be conscripted to many beliefs; much that he says is not in conflict with the Gaia hypothesis. He had, for instance, grasped that evaporation is the main reason why the oceans do not grow bigger.

I wanted to understand and absorb everything when I was young. While I was looking at the great achievements of the Renaissance painters (in photographs, of course), and reading Vasari's *Lives of the Painters*, I was also trying to digest the sorrowful facts contained in J. L. Hammond's *The Town Labourer* and *The Village Labourer*, and reading that monument of the last century, Henry Mayhew's *London Labour and the London Poor*. The grand and the mean, the victors and the vanquished.

G. B. Tiepolo is one of the great European artists. When I first looked Tiepolo up in encyclopaedias, I found him listed as representing the last decadent wave of the Renaissance. His reputation, however, has grown since then. Now he is accepted as the master of the grand rococo style – an art movement which scarcely touched Britain. At that time the English were building ugly Nonconformist churches in the depths of Norfolk and Cornwall.

I wrote a whole novel based on my imagination of Tiepolo's twilight world. Yet it could not be said he had an early influence on me. I did not know his name when I was a child. My parents did not know his name. Perhaps no one in East Dereham knew his name.

My visual sense was acute as a child. I still remember the posters that decorated the hoardings I passed on the way to my infant school. There was the terrifying Indian who advertised Moccasin Shoes. There was the jolly man in his pyjamas clinging to a giant bottle of Bovril in a rough sea ("Bovril prevents that sinking feeling"). There was the pun with the boy in an Eton suit devouring a sandwich – Percy Vere with Oxo. And there was the paradox which no youthful mind could accommodate, in which a glass and a half of milk were being poured into a single bar of Cadbury's Dairy Milk Chocolate.

How shaming to have only those two glasses of milk to remember, not the sunlit poisons of Tiepolo's heavily clad wizards, burning a serpent on a stone altar!

One pictorial element in our home gave me particular pleasure from my earliest years. H. H. Aldiss's shop, and our flat which was a part of the shop, had been redesigned after the First World War by my architect uncle, Bert Wilson, from Peterborough. In our square bay window with its comfortable window seat, he had set a little scene in stained glass. It represented Norfolk, with its gentle hills, woods, humble houses and – not least – the sea. For the first twelve years of my life, I looked at that motif every day when I was at home. Amazingly, despite all the changes, the window still exists. It is reproduced here on my title page: hardly a Tiepolo, but the sole surviving H. J. Wilson, a memorial to my dear uncle whose last words were, "The mango – a majestic fruit . . . "

As I close this account, I have cause to think of two writer friends, Arthur C. Clarke and Christopher Priest.

Arthur is over in England to receive a CBE from the Queen in the summer's honours list. He has lived for many years in Sri Lanka, which at present appears to be falling apart. Happily, the same cannot be said of Arthur. What one admires most is his sense of humour and all those visionary novels and stories (of which I still take most pleasure in the novel *Child-*

hood's End and the short story "The Nine Billion Names of God"). Beyond that sails the buoyant scientific optimism which has won him worldwide fame, untinged, unlike his old friend Heinlein, by militarism. This has never cut him off from his roots in Somerset or, for that matter, in SF. He brought out his "My Writing Life" book, *Astounding Days*, some while before this record of mine. For all the complexity of the global world in which he so successfully lives, Arthur has the gift of remaining a simple man. Long live Arthur C. Clarke, CBE!

Chris Priest has just been presented with twins, a boy and a girl, by his writer wife, Leigh Kennedy. That's better than a CBE. Chris knows it, and currently rejoices.

Unlike Clarke, Priest has travelled from fame, when he was officially reckoned one of Britain's Twenty Best Young Novelists, to a comparative obscurity, following the undeserved publishing disasters attending his complex novel, *The Glamour*. Priest is of a later generation than Clarke. On him descended all the doubts about the value of generic SF – one of the legacies of beginning a writing career when the storm of the English New Wave was raging. He has striven towards the grey area in writing between SF and accepted realism, where a man treads at his peril.

Priest is a compelling conversationalist, always clear and generally just in his judgments. Amusing, too. To my mind, he has never written enough. His presence alone has had an influence for sanity on English SF. His glittering short stories and such novels as *The Space Machine* and *Dream of Wessex* deserve to be immediately reprinted.

Like Clarke's, Priest's involvements stretch far beyond the sceptred isle of England. He has married (serially, it's true) two American wives. Clarke pioneered the communications satellite; Priest has been as adventurous, in a quiet way.

Even Clarke who, among SF writers the world over, might seem the most just target for envy, knows how many difficulties bestrew the path of a writer. Well, as Damon Runyon said, "All life is six to five against."

*   *   *

I was on a forum at a convention in New York in the early seventies. Also speaking was Barry Malzberg, then in his most productive years.

He rose to address the audience. There sat the fans of that most famous of cities, hundreds and hundreds of them.

Barry told them how writers strove against their baser selves to create something worthwhile. They strove to amuse, to please, to horrify and delight. As SF writers, they strove to tear down the curtains of the readers' imagination. They sought new ways of prose and thought. Barry is an eloquent man.

And what did writers get in return?

Nothing, said Barry.

All readers really wanted was the same old thing they had heard before. They didn't care about science or poetry or the nuances of human life. They just wanted cheap throwaway thrills. Barry laid it on thick.

You disappoint us, he told his audience. We think better of you than you think of yourselves. You don't care about us. You don't love us.

You starve us, he said. *You starve us.*

We marched out of the hall to feeble applause. It is a serious matter to be addressed by Barry Malzberg.

Outside the building, Barry's great car was waiting, dark as Pluto, long as the Ritz. He drove Margaret and me grandly through Manhattan, and took us to the best kosher restaurant in town, after which he paid the bill.

Barry, you were right, all those years ago.

They starve us, they starve us . . .

Appendix

By Nicholas Ruddick, University of Regina

THE BROOD OF MARY

Brian Aldiss, *Frankenstein*, and Science Fiction

A paper delivered to
the Ninth Conference of the Fantastic in the Arts
Fort Lauderdale, Florida, USA
March 1988

"It may be time to let *Frankenstein* illuminate our century anew. Victor and the monster can stand for the two sides of the brain. The irresponsible linear left has disinherited that which in fact it most needs, the intuitive right, its one twin in the universe best suited to rejoice in the whole brain's cognisance of nature."

Aldiss, SF as SF.

On the face of it, Brian Aldiss's *Trillion Year Spree* (1986) is an updating, with David Wingrove's help, of Aldiss's popular history of science fiction *Billion Year Spree* (1973) to include recent developments in the genre. In fact, however, the real significance of this work is that it is a massive reaffirmation by Aldiss of his controversial thesis in *Billion Year Spree* that science fiction originated with Mary Shelley's *Frankenstein*. I will not be concerned here with the objective truth of Aldiss's thesis; what I intend instead is to clarify how he arrived at it and why it continues to be so important to him.

The critical task of discovering unity in Aldiss's polymorphous fictional oeuvre is unusually difficult. As Colin Greenland has put it, "The abundance and diversity of his work, the ease with which he changes direction, make it difficult to be altogether confident in any discussion of Aldiss ... As a whole, his career has no discernible periodic structure". For this "abundance and diversity" the serious reader of science fiction has every reason to be grateful. So much of science fiction is formulaic that unpredictability is of itself refreshing. Yet unpredictability for its own sake may mask as great a conceptual vacancy as slavery to formula. If we need evidence that such circumstances do not apply in Aldiss's case, we need only turn to his critical writings, where we find a unitary voice that the fiction seems to lack. To trace Aldiss's thinking about science fiction is to discover a consistently developing project: namely, to expound a functional theory of science fiction by extending an idea to the point where it becomes so elaborate that it would be more apt to call it a myth. This myth is one of origin, and is derived from the idea that Mary Shelley's *Frankenstein* is the urtext of science fiction. But I do not mean to imply by "myth" that Aldiss is guilty, consciously or otherwise, of embracing a fallacy. He is well aware of the strength of arguments that uphold other origins for science fiction. However, for his purposes – and, he feels, ultimately for the purposes of all serious readers of science fiction – Mary Shelley is a far more appropriate originator of a literature of the significance that science fiction ought to have than Lucian of Samosata, H. G. Wells, Hugo Gernsback or any of the other popular candidates for founding father.

I will trace Aldiss's thinking about science fiction in general and *Frankenstein* in particular in his critical writings and in the novel that bears directly on the topic at hand, *Frankenstein Unbound*. I hope to show that far more than a vague line of influence connects Aldiss to the author of *Frankenstein*. That Mary Shelley flourished in the Romantic era, that she was a woman, and that she was British are all crucial factors in Aldiss's formulation of what has certainly been the most influential functional theory of science fiction to date.

The Shape of Further Things (1970), subtitled *Speculation on Change*, is a deliberately unfocused collection of short essays by a self-confessed "amateur thinker" at what he perceives to be a historical watershed. Aldiss begins by stating bluntly that "Western man has achieved his staggering technological success by maiming himself". The result is that Western civilisation "is, under its own impetus, heading towards a new technological barbarism". The maiming is the result of an overdevelopment of the head, seat of the intellect, at the expense of the heart, seat of the emotions. The artist's present task is to remedy this imbalance. As the schism between head and heart corresponds to that between science and art, the science fiction writer, whose very title embraces this latter duality, is particularly well qualified to perform the urgent task of integration: "in their origins, art and science were interfused, inseparable; good science fiction writers seek to make them whole again".

Other corresponding dualities occur to Aldiss, especially that represented on the one hand by the airy *Scherzi* ("Jokes"), a set of etchings by the Venetian artist G. B. Tiepolo (1696-1770), and on the other by the gloomy engravings known as the *Carceri* ("Prisons") by his contemporary G. Piranesi (1720-78). Admiring both works, Aldiss identifies the former with Shakespeare's ethereal spirit Ariel and the latter with the powerful earthbound Caliban. He concludes that "The future offers none of the lightness and magic of Tiepolo; we are heading instead for one of Piranesi's prisons!" Beyond this set of dualities lies another, that represented by the relationship between waking reality and dream, and here we return to the science fiction writer as mediator:

> Science fiction is a particular form of fantasy; although, with regard to form and expression, it generally clings to a somewhat faded realism, in content it comes remarkably close to dream, combining as it does both ancient and modern myth-ingredients.

The Shape of Further Things concludes with an appendix in which Dr Christopher Evans outlines his "functional" theory of dreaming. This theory uses the analogy of a computer placed off-line to reclassify useful and discard useless information, to explain how the brain organises the day's experience by various processes of storing and discarding memories, of which dreaming is the most important. For Aldiss, the theory itself suggests a functional theory of science fiction. Just as the apparently irrational dream is essential to the well-being of the brain, so science fiction is, or should be, essential to the health of Western technocracy. The good science fiction writer's aim should be to mediate between the "reality" of the head and the "fantasy" of the heart in a culture which tends to privilege the former in a way that, if unchecked, can only lead to catastrophe.

But this grand functional theory of science fiction is only present embryonically in *The Shape of Further Things*. What is still lacking is evidence that science fiction really does mediate between the alienated hemispheres of our schizophrenic culture. Aldiss's next task was to identify that time in cultural history when the split took place and to locate there the probable origin of science fiction. After all, if science fiction is an act of integration, it must have begun as a response to

212

disintegration. The proto-Romantic, or Gothic, *Carceri* are for Aldiss an early foreshadowing of the nightmarish path Western civilisation was to follow. With Piranesi, the Enlightenment ends and the clouds begin to gather – a process continuing relentlessly today. Indeed, at the end of *The Shape of Further Things* Aldiss refers to future space colonists as "benighted children of the Enlightenment". We might already guess, then, that for Aldiss the urtext of science fiction would almost inevitably spring from the post-Enlightenment generation, from someone who shared the Gothic sensibility of Piranesi, who understood that humanity stood on a darkling plain and who strove to understand how this state of affairs had come about.

Billion Year Spree and *Frankenstein Unbound*, both published in 1973, are two different articulations of the same discovery: that of the origin of the science-fictional species. In the former we are told that science fiction springs from "the dream world of the Gothic novel", Gothic being a fictional subgenre that is itself a response to the failure of Enlightenment thought. Moreover, to this day science fiction is "characteristically cast in the Gothic or post-Gothic mould". The first true science fiction novel is Mary Shelley's *Frankenstein* (1818), "the first novel to be powered by evolution"; that is, by the body of scientific theory that finally broke the already weakened grip of religious doctrine on Western culture. That *Frankenstein* predates Darwin's *Origin of Species* (1859) by over forty years is no objection, for Mary Shelley was immersed in proto-evolutionary thought. Moreover, her novel achieves a balance between the "Outwardness of Science and society" (which we might identify with the head/intellect/reality nexus) and the "Inwardness" deriving from the oneiric origin of the novel and giving it its "psychological depth". That *Frankenstein* has become a "new myth" – something difficult to deny – confirms that it offered a way of comprehending an unprecedented human predicament that those coming after could build upon; hence Aldiss's claim that the novel originated a literary genre.

213

Yet Aldiss's thesis about the origin of science fiction is founded on more than his admiration for *Frankenstein*'s literary qualities and his sense of the novel's historical importance. The dynamic of the thesis is what can only be called a special relationship between Aldiss and Mary Shelley, which first comes into focus in the novel *Frankenstein Unbound*. It is set in the near future in which, as a metaphor of present psychic and cultural disintegration, space and time have gone "on the blink" as a result of stratospheric nuclear tests. A London *Times* leader, endorsed by the novel's narrator Joseph Bodenland, spells out the significance of what has happened:

> We can no longer rely even on the sane sequence of temporal progression; tomorrow may prove to be last week, or last century, or the Age of the Pharaohs. The Intellect has made our planet unsafe for intellect. We are suffering from the curse that was Baron Frankenstein's in Mary Shelley's novel: by seeking to control too much, we have lost control of ourselves.

Using Aldiss's own terminology, we might decode this as follows: Frankenstein's curse is visited upon those who privilege the head over the heart,[1] and takes the form of a dissolution of those verities (represented by space and time in the novel) without which human life ceases to have a meaning; self-destruction inevitably follows.

Bodenland is a mouthpiece[2] for the Aldiss of *The Shape of Further Things*. But he is more: as an American (he is a former presidential adviser) he embodies the current dynamic of Western technocracy. A thoughtful liberal, Bodenland has recently fallen from grace with the administration, which

,1
[1] "Breakdowns are almost always caused by a victory of head over heart [in Aldiss's fiction] (it is no accident that Frankenstein's first name is Victor)" (Mathews, p.53).

[2] Mathew's term is "spokesman" (p.52).

suggests that the humane qualities he possesses are no longer valued. He timeslips into Geneva in May 1816, but a Geneva in which Mary Shelley and her fictional creations coexist. Observing Dr Frankenstein at work, Bodenland sees clearly how the "plague virus", that is the scientist's need to set nature to rights by interfering with human mortality, has been passed on, ever increasing in virulence, to Bodenland's own age – which is now infected to the point of collapse. The equation is clear: "The Conquest of Nature – the loss of man's inner self!" The result is also clear: loss of inner self leads to psychic and cultural disintegration. That this disintegration should be symbolised by timeslips is apt, for Western man has tried to impose a "confining straightness" on time; while natural time is far more wayward, "like Mary Shelley's reputation". Before Bodenland can begin to understand the lesson of 1816, he must shed his watch.[3]

The sexual idyll between Bodenland and Mary Shelley in Chapter Nine dramatises the desire for the integration of dualities which permeates Aldiss's critical project. In it, albeit briefly, male and female, fictional and real, are united. If Bodenland is a liberal American technocrat, Mary Shelley embodies the radical English literary tradition. From their union springs science fiction, a form of literature that shares the thoughtful and radical qualities of its parents and which alone can properly confront the cultural predicament of the twentieth century. What are by implication excluded from this union are on the one hand technology-worshipping American pulp science fiction, and on the other the genteel English conservative literary tradition, represented by what Aldiss refers to in *The Shape of Further Things* as "English literary gentlemen [who] hate all [H. G.] Wells stood for". For preceding Aldiss's integrative project is a necessary deconstructive one: he gives priority to the female Mary Shelley over the patriarchs of science fiction, and priority to

[3] For the importance of time in the novel, see McNelly, pp.840-4.

215

the English Mary Shelley over the American pulpsters.

Is it fair to say that there is such a close identification between the author of *Frankenstein Unbound* and his narrator that, as Patrick G. McLeod has put it, "we sense a vicarious wish-fulfilment for Aldiss" in the sexual idyll? I think it is, if this is not taken to mean that we are being offered merely a private fantasy. In fact, the desire of which the idyll is the fulfilment is identical to that motivating Aldiss's critical project, as David Wingrove has made clear:

> *Frankenstein Unbound* is, ultimately, as so many of Aldiss's novels are, a search for integration – for that reconciliation of the head and the heart he discusses in [*The*] *Shape* [*of Further Things*]: the union of Yin and Yang, of male and female principles.

In *Frankenstein Unbound* Aldiss has created an alternate world in which his time-torn surrogate, Bodenland, comes to discover the nature of his psychological and cultural predicament through knowledge, in both the epistemological and biblical senses of the word, of Mary Shelley, the woman who first warned the children of the Enlightenment that the monster had been unbound. The documents relating Bodenland's experiences are "really" a science fiction novel by Brian Aldiss, a novel paradigmatic right down to the "post-Gothic-mould" of Aldiss's actual definition of science fiction in *Billion Year Spree* and of his implied definition of science fiction as a literary mode[4] that ought to try to bridge the divided self of Western civilisation.

As yet the most complete articulation of Aldiss's functional theory of science fiction is his pamphlet *Science Fiction as Science Fiction* (1978). What is new here is his replacement of the head/heart duality with one based on the bicameral physiology of the brain:

---

[4] See *Trillion*, p.19, for Aldiss's change from "mould" to "mode".

My proposal . . . is that SF is an ideal negotiator between the two hemispheres of the brain, the rational cognitive – i.e. "scientific" – left and the intuitive, i.e. "literary-artistic" – right; so its proper function is to cleave closely neither to science nor literature.

Aldiss's corollary to this is that though he believes "that SF is a pursuit for rational men", any science fiction which favours too greatly the left hemisphere becomes "propaganda"; while favouring the irrational right gives rise to "LF"– the world of Erich von Daniken, the Bermuda Triangle and Uri Geller.

Two other significant elements are added to the Frankensteinian myth of origin in this pamphlet. The first is that, for Aldiss, *Frankenstein* is the work that best discloses the "prodromic function of SF . . . it can frequently act . . . as a symptom of something forthcoming, perhaps unknown to the author – simply because it is . . . near to the things that are real". In *Frankenstein Unbound*, Mary Shelley was a female object of desire offering knowledge through possession for the male author-surrogate; now she had become woman as Sybil or Pythian, at once more intuitive and more earthy – more in touch with the "real" – than a man. In the complicated scheme reproduced in the pamphlet, "Prodroma" (which means something like "having the quality of being premonitory") is the bridging function between Left Hemispheric Prediction and Right Hemispheric Wishing. On the vertical axis it falls between "TRUTH" and what is for Aldiss another central work of female science fiction, Anna Kavan's *Ice*.

"Mary Wollstonecraft Shelley" (1982), an essay revised under the title "Science Fiction's Mother Figure," clarifies the importance for Aldiss of Mary Shelley's womanhood. "Only a woman, only Mary Shelley, could have written *Frankenstein*", he asserts. This is because she knew far more about "life" than her male contemporaries. What she knew was the "fear, guilt, depression, and anxiety" of childbearing while she was the consort of "a married man with children by another woman, and beset by debt in a foreign place". Moreover, her character had been initiated into hard knowledge about life by her childhood: "Her reserved manner hid deep feelings baffled by her mother's death shortly after Mary's birth and her father's distance." The monster is not only "mankind itself, blundering about the world seeking knowledge and reassurance", but also Mary Shelley, an exile born from the dead who failed to win acceptance into society: "Part of the continued appeal of the novel is the appeal of the drama of the neglected child."

The essay "A Monster for All Seasons" (1982), in which Aldiss also deals specifically with *Frankenstein*, reveals why he feels that the question of science fiction's origin is so "wrapped up with" the question of its function:

> To regard SF as existing in literature since Homer is to bestow on it no function not also operative in literature; which contradicts the experience of most of us who study and enjoy both literature and SF.
>
> To regard SF as "all starting with Gernsback" is to impoverish it unfairly. SF then becomes a kind of gadget fiction, where every story more than ten years old is hailed as a "Classic", and reputations can be made by rewriting one's previous story ad infinitum.

Here Aldiss insists on the difference between literature and science fiction, with good science fiction positively subversive of the realistic mode that characterises the fictional mainstream. Science fiction's special task is to find "an objective correlative for the cold intellectual currents" of the industrial age. *Frankenstein* was the first great myth of this age, and as such is the urtext of science fiction.

But there is something more still. Mary Shelley's sense of alienation, that so powerfully emerges in both her life story and in her "autobiographical" novel *Frankenstein*, is felt as keenly by the author of *Frankenstein Unbound*. This we can see clearly if we turn to Aldiss's own autobiographical writings.

In "Magic and Bare Boards" (1975) he notes how (just like a benighted child of the Enlightenment) he "lost hope in the idea of Reason as a guiding light". Having left his childhood home, he "never belonged anywhere again" – with the possible exception of science fiction fandom, where the brood of Mary gather, perhaps for the most part unwittingly, to celebrate their great Mother. Elsewhere he states that "the love of art and science I developed as a child was a rebellion against the smug *bourgeois* society in which I found myself" ("Monster"). Moreover, his "abrupt uprooting in early childhood" (*This World*) is something he shares with Asimov, Nerval, Wells, Stapledon, Ballard and, of course, Mary Shelley. Finally, in his moving autobiographical piece "The Glass Forest" (1986), he discloses what is perhaps the key to his identification with Mary Shelley:

> In concluding this sketch, I cannot but note that there is much pain in it. So there is in any truthful autobiographical account. For many years I was unable to deal with the pain I experienced, and unable to communicate it. Like Frankenstein's monster, I felt malicious because I was miserable – the very reverse of Christian doctrine. And my difficulty was the monster's – parental coldness. (*And the Lurid*).

For Aldiss, then, Mary Shelley is as mythic as her own creations. She is the female counterpart of the otherwise incomplete male author, whose desire to know her is a desire for wholeness in a time characterised by increasing and potentially catastrophic psychic and cultural disintegration. She is at once an embodiment of the eternal Mother, whom our left-hemispheric culture has tried to erase but whom the lost and benighted children of the Enlightenment must finally acknowledge if they are to survive. As Mother, she gave birth to that myth that most directly confronts our modern predicament, thus preparing the way for a literary genre, science fiction, that alone of the literary arts has the ability to bridge the alienated hemispheres of our divided selves and set up a dialogue between them. Finally, as inheritor from both her parents of the radical English literary tradition, she ensures the intellectual authority – though perhaps not the respectability – of the genre she founded. Aldiss's complex and deeply felt relationship with Mary Shelley offers itself finally as a paradigm of how seriously and passionately science fiction ought to engage those who work within the genre.

WORKS CITED

Aldiss, Brian. *And the Lurid Glare of the Comet*, Serconia Press, Seattle, 1986.

—. *Billion Year Spree: The History of Science Fiction*, London, 1973; Corgi, 1975.

—. *Frankenstein Unbound*, London, 1973; Triad/Granada, 1982.

—. "Magic and Bare Boards", *Hell's Cartographers: Some Personal Histories of Science Fiction Writers*. Eds. Brian Aldiss and Harry Harrison, London, 1975; Futura, 1976, pp.179-209.

—. "Mary Wollstonecraft Shelley", *Science Fiction Writers*, Ed. E. F. Bleiler, Scribner's, New York, 1982. Rptd as "Science Fiction's Mother Figure", *The Pale Shadow of Science*, Serconia Press, Seattle, 1985, pp.37-49.

—. *Science Fiction as Science Fiction*, Bran's Head, UK, 1978.

—. *The Shape of Further Things: Speculation on Change*, London, 1970; Corgi, 1974.

—. *This World and Nearer Ones: Essays Exploring the Familiar*, Weidenfeld, London, 1979.

—. with David Wingrove, *Trillion Year Spree: The History of Science Fiction*, Gollancz, London, 1986.

Aldiss, Margaret. *The Work of Brian W. Aldiss: an annotated bibliography and guide*, Borgo, San Bernardino, California, 1990.

Greenland, Colin. *The Entropy Exhibition: Michael Moorcock and the British "New Wave" in Science Fiction*, Routledge, London, 1983.

Griffin, Brian and David Wingrove. *Apertures: A Study of the Writings of Brian W. Aldiss*, Greenwood Press, Westport and London, 1984.

McLeod, Patrick G. "Frankenstein: Unbound and Otherwise", *Extrapolation* 21 (1980), pp.158-66.

Mathews, Richard. *Aldiss Unbound: The Science Fiction of Brian W. Aldiss*, Borgo, San Bernadino, 1977.

McNelly, Willis E. *"Frankenstein Unbound"*, Survey of Science Fiction Literature, Ed. Frank N. Magill, Salem Press, Englewood Cliffs, 1979, pp.840-44.